Liquidation of Empire

Liquidation of Empire

The Decline of the British Empire

Roy Douglas

First published 2002 by
PALGRAVE MACMILLAN
Houndmills, Basingstoke, Hampshire RG21 6XS and
175 Fifth Avenue, New York, N.Y. 10010
Companies and representatives throughout the world

PALGRAVE MACMILLAN is the global academic imprint of the Palgrave
Macmillan division of St Martin's Press, LLC and of Palgrave Macmillan Ltd.
Macmillan® is a registered trademark in the United States, United Kingdom
and other countries. Palgrave is a registered trademark in the European
Union and other countries.

ISBN 0-333-80454-6

This book is printed on paper suitable for recycling and
made from fully managed and sustained forest sources.

A catalogue record for this book is available
from the British Library.

Library of Congress Cataloging-in-Publication Data
Douglas, Roy, 1924-
    Liquidation of empire: the decline of the British Empire / Roy Douglas.
    p. cm.
    Includes bibliographical references and index.
    ISBN 0–333–80454–6
    1. Great Britain–Colonies–History–20th century. 2.
Decolonization–Great Britain–Colonies–History–20th century. 3.
Imperialism–Government policy–Great Britain–History–20th century. 4.
Commonwealth countries– History–20th century. I. Title.

DA16 .D68 2002
909'.09712410825–dc21   2002019599

10 9 8 7 6 5 4 3 2
11 10 09 08 07 06 05 04

Printed and bound in Great Britain by
Antony Rowe Ltd, Chippenham and Eastbourne

Contents

Acknowledgements

I am deeply grateful to my wife Jean who worked through the manuscript and made many helpful suggestions. She is not an historian, and that has been particularly useful, since this book is aimed at a popular as well as a professional readership. The map on p. viii is from Martin Gilbert, *The Dent Atlas of British History*, and is reproduced by kind permission of Taylor and Francis.

The British Empire 1920

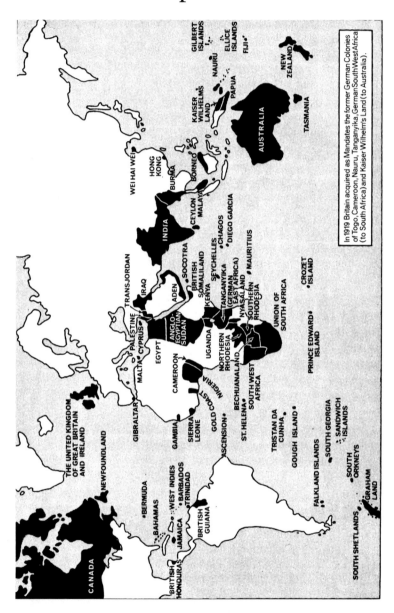

In 1919 Britain acquired as Mandates the former German Colonies of Togo, Cameroon, Nauru, Tanganyika, GermanSouthWestAfrica (to South Africa) and Kaiser Wilhelm's Land (to Australia).

1
Zenith

On 10 November 1942, Winston Churchill told the House of Commons: 'I have not become the King's First Minister in order to preside over the liquidation of the British Empire.' Five years earlier George Orwell, very much a man of the 'Left', had reflected that 'at the bottom of his heart, no Englishman ... does want [the Empire] to disintegrate'.[1]

When Churchill spoke, children at school still celebrated Queen Victoria's birthday, 24 May, as 'Empire Day', when they were encouraged to reflect on the merits and durability of the British Empire, and received a half-holiday in the afternoon to give the occasion a pleasant flavour. Many people who had profound qualms about the way in which that Empire had been acquired, and even about the wisdom of acquiring an Empire at all, would still have acknowledged that speedy 'liquidation' would do much damage, not only to Britain but to the remainder of the Empire as well. And yet, by the time of Churchill's death in 1965, the British Empire had all but ceased to exist.

What happened, and why? In 1945, Britain emerged victorious from the greatest war of history, universally acknowledged as one of the 'Big Three' countries which would play the dominant part in determining the future of the world. The other two members of the trio may have looked askance at the British Empire for disparate reasons; but neither was disposed at that moment to play an active part in destroying it.

The present study examines the 'liquidation' process mainly from the 'official' British point of view. In the nineteenth century, and even down to the immediate aftermath of the 1914–18 war, British governments had often sought to extend the bounds of the Empire; so what persuaded them to do the very reverse in the later part of the twentieth century?

In 1914, the British Empire encompassed roughly a quarter of the world's land and population. From Britain's point of view, the Empire performed various functions. Some of these were essentially economic. Thus, India and the West African countries were sources of goods which could not be produced in Britain. No doubt most, if not all, of those goods could be obtained from places which were not part of the British Empire; but there were often impediments on trade with countries outside the Empire. Other functions were largely social. Many British people who thought that their personal prospects were cramped at home went to the Empire, either to carve out a career or in the hope of living there permanently. Some territories, like Malta and Gibraltar, were held for strategic reasons; others as useful 'coaling stations' on important sea routes. Some had been acquired at times when their likely value was uncertain, in order to get a foot in the door before another Power arrived. Many Empire-builders had sought personal gain, and often they had acted with great brutality; while others had been inspired, and continued to be inspired, by a sincere desire to assist the local people: to convert them to Christianity; or to introduce them to a 'civilised' way of life; or to improve their economic conditions.

The British Empire was never controlled by a single Department of State. The Foreign Office was responsible for relations with what might be called 'semi-Empire' countries like Egypt. India was the responsibility of the India Office. The Colonies came under the Colonial Office. Later, a separate Dominions Office, and eventually a Commonwealth Relations Office, was set up to deal with self-governing territories.[2]

Broadly, the Empire was expected to pay its way, and the amount of money available for Imperial development was small. In many places, administration was largely controlled by 'traditional' authorities like local chiefs. In others, British officials were responsible; but Britons were present in astonishingly small numbers, and the task of running components of the Empire fell largely on local people. In Africa, 'on the eve of the Second World War, the élite administrative division of the Civil Service ... numbered slightly more than 1,200 men ... spread over more than a dozen colonies [with an] estimated population of 43 millions'.[3] In India, the position was similar. In the last year of British rule, Prime Minister Attlee reminded a senior minister:

> We have always governed India through the Indians. Without tens of thousands of lesser functionaries we could not carry on. In a typical district of one or two million [it is quite common for there to be] only one or two white officials.[4]

In 1914, the member-countries of the Empire were at very different stages of political development. At one end of the spectrum were the places which soon came to be called 'Dominions' – Canada, Australia, New Zealand, South Africa and Newfoundland (then separate from Canada). One writer has noted that

> the Dominions enjoyed virtually complete self-government in all domestic matters; they ordered, directly or indirectly, their constitutions; their parliaments legislated within their borders without interference from London; they drew up their tariffs; they regulated their immigration; they had their own military and naval forces subject to their own control.[5]

At the other extreme of political development were tiny island colonies, with populations numbered in hundreds or at most in thousands, which neither possessed nor sought powers of self-government. Between those two extremes were colonies at various stages of independence. The larger colonies often had Executive and Legislative Councils, some of which were composed only of officials and nominees of the colonial Governor, while in other places several members of the Legislative Council were directly elected. The electorate, however, was usually composed mainly or entirely of members of the white population.

In addition to the Colonies, in the strict sense of the word, there were many 'Protectorates'. Just what constituted a Protectorate was not always clear; but, roughly, one may say that it was a territory controlled largely by local people, but where Britain had overriding power, which was recognised internationally. Often Colonies and Protectorates were closely linked. Thus, the southern part of the

Gold Coast was a Colony, but the Ashanti region and the northern region ranked as Protectorates. The Governor appointed from London was responsible for Colony and Protectorates alike. Protectorates could be 'annexed', and become Colonies. Thus, in 1920 what had formerly been known as the East African Protectorate became Kenya Colony.

India, by far the most populous part of the British Empire, followed rules all of its own, and this point was recognised in the special status of the sovereign. For the remainder of the British Empire, he was King; but he was Emperor of India. The Indian Empire at that time included also modern Pakistan, Bangladesh and Myanmar (Burma). Various systems of government operated. The 'Princely States', or 'Native States', which were numbered in hundreds, were rather like protectorates. They ranged in size from tiny territories of a few square miles to Hyderabad, whose area was roughly the same as Great Britain, and whose population was around 13 million. These 'Princely States' were linked with 'British India' by various treaties and enjoyed varying degrees of autonomy.

'British India', whose population formed something like four-fifths of the whole, was divided into large Provinces. The Secretary of State for India was normally a member of the British Cabinet and was assisted by a Council of India, with special powers over finance. The head of government in India itself was the Viceroy, sometimes called the Governor-General. He was appointed, usually for five years, on recommendation of the British Government, and assisted by an Executive Council, in some ways comparable with a British Cabinet. There had never been, and there never was to be, an Indian appointed to the office of Viceroy. It was even accounted remarkable in 1909 when the first Indian was appointed to the Viceroy's Executive Council. There was also a much bigger Legislative Council, which included some *ex officio* members, some nominated members and some who were elected by a rather narrow Indian electorate. In the period immediately before the outbreak of war in 1914, John Morley, Secretary of State for India, actively encouraged increased Indian representation at all levels of government.

The overwhelming majority of senior posts in the Indian Civil Service was held by Europeans, although at lower levels Indians predominated. About a third of the Indian Army, which had a peacetime establishment of around 250,000, was composed of Europeans. Yet if all Britons in the civil and military administration of India were put together, they probably amounted to not much more than 100,000 persons, who between them played the major part in governing a country whose population at the time was more than 300 million. The 1914 war witnessed remarkable changes in several important parts of the British Empire. In general, the Dominions acted for practical purposes like sovereign Powers. The southern Dominions 'conducted their own military expeditions, occupied enemy territory, and, when successful, decided on terms of capitulation, without any interference from Great Britain'.[6] Only in one Dominion were there serious signs of disaffection during the 1914 war, and that, not surprisingly, was South Africa. The Union of South Africa had been founded in 1910 by bringing together two British colonies, the Cape and Natal, and the two Boer states, the Transvaal and the Orange Free State, which had been annexed at the end of the South African (or Boer) War of 1899–1902. In contrast with the other Dominions, people of non-European stock formed the large majority of the population of South Africa, although they had little power.

South Africa's participation in the war of 1914 had been supported by most of the English-speaking population, but the Boers were deeply divided. Many of them, including two of the most famous Boer Generals of the South African War, Louis Botha and Jan Smuts, played important parts in the Allied cause. At the other extreme, Christian De Wet, another celebrated General of the Boer War period, took the declaration of war in 1914 as occasion to launch a military insurrection in South Africa. The rising failed, and the insurgents were treated with wise compassion in the aftermath; but it served as an important warning that not all Boers had been reconciled to the Imperial link.

In India, there were few immediate signs of trouble when war came. The great majority of those Indians who were capable of expressing any views on the matter gave strong support to the British cause. The main Indian doubts about the war were expressed after Turkey became a belligerent on the German side a few months later. Some Muslims felt a religious loyalty to the Ottoman Sultan in his capacity as Caliph, or Successor, to the Prophet. Most Indians, including many Muslims, do not appear to have shared such doubts. After all, far more Muslims lived in India than in Turkey, or any other country in the world.

As the war continued, complaints of various kinds arose. In June 1917, Austen Chamberlain, Secretary of State for India in Lloyd George's Coalition Government, expressed what the Cabinet minutes described as 'grave anxiety'[7] about 'the rapidity with which events were moving in India, and ... the accelerated progress of thought in that country. There was a rapid surface current of advanced political feeling, which ... was bound to permeate to the hitherto unstirred deeps below.' It was urgently necessary, declared Chamberlain, for the Government 'to come forward at once and declare publicly that their ultimate aim – distant though the realisation of that aim might be – was self-government'. A few weeks later, the Conservative (or, technically, 'Unionist') Chamberlain was succeeded as Secretary for India by the Liberal Edwin Montagu, who raised the matter in a very similar vein to his predecessor. The Cabinet adopted a formula, deriving from the former Viceroy, Lord Curzon, that

> the policy of His Majesty's Government is that of the increasing association of Indians in every branch of the administration, and the gradual development of self-governing institutions, with a view to the progressive realisation of responsible government in India under the aegis of the British Crown.[8]

Thus Britain was committed to the eventual attainment of something very similar to what people later called 'Dominion status' for India.

After the war ended, the victorious Allies, acting through the newly-formed League of Nations, decided to grant 'Mandates' over former German colonies and over non-Turkish parts of the Ottoman Empire to particular countries. These Mandates were not to be colonies in the old sense of the term, but were held on trust for the League. Britain received Mandates over some Ottoman lands, which will call for much attention later, and also over a number of former German colonies.

The Dominions sent their own delegations to the Peace Conference and signed the Treaties in their own right. Three of them received Mandates over former German colonies, under auspices of the League. South Africa received the Mandate over South-West Africa (now Namibia), Australia over German New Guinea, and New Zealand over Samoa. The Pacific island of Nauru was given as a joint Mandate to Britain, Australia and New Zealand. These Mandates provided a remarkable indication of the way in which the Dominions were becoming regarded, not only by Britain but by other nations as well, as sovereign states for most purposes.

The immediate aftermath of the 1914 war saw some very serious rumblings in parts of the British Empire. Two countries, Ireland and India, were of particular importance in this respect, and there is much to be said for the view that what happened in those places in that period would prove of critical importance for the whole process of imperial 'liquidation'. In both countries, those events had deep roots.

Since 1801, Ireland had formed an integral part of the United Kingdom, sending rather more than 100 MPs to the House of Commons. Many Irish people, however, considered that this 'union' was in practice a mere euphemism for domination of a smaller, weaker Ireland by British political and economic interests. In the nineteenth century, a strong movement for Irish 'Home Rule' came into existence. Home Rule would certainly entail establishment of an Irish Parliament in Dublin, with control over specifically Irish affairs; but how much further Home Rule was meant to go in the direction of separation was by no means clear. By the 1880s, Irish attitudes to union had come to follow fairly closely the lines of religion. The overwhelming majority of Catholics favoured a greater or lesser measure of Home Rule; while most Protestants were Unionists: that is, they favoured retention of the existing union.

Long before 1914, the question of Home Rule *versus* continuing union with Britain was the dominant public issue in Ireland, and for much of the time it was the dominant issue in Britain as well. Just before the outbreak of war, a Bill to grant Home Rule to Ireland was ready for the King's signature, which would be given as a matter of course. Provision was made in the Bill for excluding the most strongly Unionist parts of Ireland from operation of Home Rule for a period of six years; but neither Unionists nor Home Rulers contemplated any kind of permanent partition in Ireland. As Home Rule had been such a controversial matter, operation of the Bill was suspended for the duration of the war, in the interest of 'national unity'.

At first, all significant Irish parties, Home Rulers and Unionists alike, supported the prosecution of the war. As that war proceeded, however, great changes took place. In April 1916, a group of Irishmen inaugurated a rising in Dublin. They had no support outside the ranks of extremists and were roundly condemned by Nationalists. By an incredible act of folly, the British Government decided in the aftermath to authorise the execution of the ringleaders, thus immediately according them the status of martyrs. Thereafter, Sinn Féin, a movement which sought to establish a sovereign Irish Republic and break all links with Britain, began to make great headway. No doubt sheer war-weariness, as well as sympathy with the executed rebels, played an important part. Immediately after the Armistice, a General Election was called in the United Kingdom, at which Sinn Féin captured a large majority of Irish seats, almost wiping out the Irish Nationalist Party, which had been the principal advocate of Home Rule in the old sense of the term.

The country soon collapsed into civil war between Irish people seeking independence on one side and the British Government authorities on the other. A kind of settlement developed in stages during 1921–22. The southern part of Ireland became the Irish Free State, which received complete internal self-government, but continued to acknowledge the King and remained part of the British Empire. The most Protestant area of Ulster remained part of the United Kingdom, under the name Northern Ireland, and continued to send MPs to Westminster; but received its own Parliament for domestic affairs.

This solution was, at best, an uneasy compromise, which did not correspond with the real wishes of any of the main groups concerned, British or Irish, Northern or Southern, Protestant or Catholic. Some British Unionist politicians were deeply hesitant; while the Irish Dáil accepted it by only a small majority. In the Free State, the agreement was soon followed by another civil war, in which Catholic Irishmen who reluctantly accepted the Free State compromise fought against Catholic Irishmen who rejected it and demanded an immediate Republic. The Free Staters won; but the legacy of bitterness was great.

There was also serious trouble in India in the immediate aftermath of the 1914–18 war. A chain of events which took place in the short period between the Armistice and signature of the first peace treaty would play a major part in turning Indian opinion against the British rule. With tragic irony, these events took place in the Punjab, an area of northern India which had been particularly generous in the supply of troops during the war.[9] The focus was the town Amritsar, the great centre of the Sikhs, a religious body whose loyal service during the war had been particularly impressive. There had been special wartime legislation to suppress possible sedition in India. When the war ended, measures commonly known as the Rowlatt Acts were introduced in the Legislative Council, designed to continue the emergency regulations into peacetime. Passage of the Rowlatt Acts was one of the factors, but by no means the only one,[10] that led to a number of outbreaks of violence in Amritsar, early in April 1919. Later in the month, a large, but unarmed, protest meeting of Indians was held there. Without warning, the British officer in charge, Brigadier-General R.E.H. Dyer, ordered troops to fire, and firing continued for ten minutes. In the end, close on 400 Indians had been killed and three times that number injured. Montagu ordered an inquiry to be held in India. Dyer was severely censured and relieved of his command.

Later in 1919, the British Parliament enacted important constitutional reforms for India, often known as the Montagu–Chelmsford reforms – Lord Chelmsford being the Viceroy. The Executive Council was to contain at least three Indian members, while the Supreme Legislative Council was to be divided into two Houses, in each of which elected representatives would form the large majority of members.

The electorate, however, would be confined to people with educational or property qualifications, and formed only a tiny minority of the population. Fewer than one million Indians would be permitted to vote for the central legislature, although about five million could vote for provincial legislatures. A system known as dyarchy was introduced for the individual Provinces. Some Departments of State came under control of ministers responsible to Provincial Executive Councils, while others came under officials appointed by the Provincial government.

Nobody regarded the Montagu–Chelmsford reforms as the end of the road; but they may be seen as signs of a real willingness to move in the direction of eventual Indian self-government. This idea of independence became increasingly attractive to educated Indians. When elections were held under the new constitution, the Swaraj, or Home Rule, Party became an important element in the Legislative Council and in Provincial Legislatures.

Some remarkable events in the early autumn of 1922 represent what might be considered the last kick of the Great War itself. These events had important consequences for both British domestic politics and the wider affairs of Empire. By the Treaty of Sèvres, concluded with the Allies in 1920, Turkey was required to make massive territorial concessions. The Treaty, however, was never ratified. War eventually developed between the Greeks and Turks, during which the Greek Army occupied the Anatolian city of Smyrna (Izmir), which had a largely Greek population. In September 1922, the town was seized by the Turks and horrendous massacres took place. Allied troops were already stationed on the approaches to Constantinople, and these included a substantial British contingent at Chanak (Çanakkale). The Coalition Government in Britain responded to the mounting crisis by taking the decision to reinforce troops at Chanak.

Telegrams were sent to the Dominions, asking them also to provide reinforcements.[11] New Zealand and Newfoundland gave swift and favourable replies. The Australian Prime Minister made a speech some days later, which the British Government considered helpful.[12] The Canadian government, however, was more hesitant, the reply indicating 'that in their opinion public opinion would require parliamentary approval before definite assistance could be sent'.[13]

Indian reactions to the Chanak episode presented special problems. Muslim members of the Indian legislature telegraphed the British Government, counselling strict neutrality and appealing for the restoration of Anglo-Turkish friendship. So the tacit assumption that a British lead on diplomatic and military matters would be followed almost automatically throughout the Empire had broken down. In the next few years, it would prove necessary to offer a definition of imperial relations which was very different from what had seemed to be the state of affairs before the war.

It would be wrong, however, to think that the Empire was already beginning to disintegrate. Except in Ireland and South Africa and – just possibly – in India, there was no substantial body of opinion which contemplated breaking away from the British Empire. In so far as force was required for the maintenance of imperial peace, this was readily available.

Yet some general lessons were plain. The 1914 war had been, on balance, a great misfortune for Britain and for her Empire. The new acquisitions from the 'Ottoman succession' would prove an almost unmitigated curse; the new acquisitions from Germany a very dubious and temporary asset. As far as India was concerned, the wise constitutional advances consequential on the 1917 declaration and the Act which followed two years later were counterposed by the disruptions and tensions which were fostered in the aftermath of war. In Ireland, a chain of events had started, which would eventually drive most of the country out of the Empire altogether and would hamper its orderly development for a very long time to come. In South Africa, old wounds had been reopened.

One forecast could be made with confidence. If Britain were to become involved in another war, much graver tensions would be set up within the Empire, whatever the outcome of the conflict might be. If Britain really believed in the unique value of her Empire not only to herself but to the other member-countries, then she must at all costs avoid war. Britain might be an imperial Power outside Europe or she might be a major force within Europe. She could not be both.

2
Uneasy Peace

Unfortunately, external events did not permit the British Empire to continue on the lines of peaceful, uninterrupted development which were essential for its future success. The astonishing Coalition Government headed by Lloyd George collapsed suddenly and unexpectedly in October 1922, and for several years to come British politics were more than usually fluid. There was much rhetoric about Empire; but in practice a wide consensus existed. None of the three parties contemplated imperial disruption, while none of them was disposed to resist substantial changes taking place if a sufficient head of steam was generated in the countries concerned. As for the Empire countries, they appeared to have settled down, more or less, from the upheavals of war and its immediate aftermath.

For a variety of reasons, many people considered that it was necessary to define the links between member-countries of the Empire more closely than had been attempted in the past. Since Victoria's 1887 Jubilee, there had been occasional conferences involving Britain and other major parts of the Empire. The Imperial Conference of 1926 paid particular attention to constitutional questions. A Committee on Inter-Imperial Relations was set up, headed by the sometime Prime Minister Earl Balfour. The Committee saw evidence of a great deal of misunderstanding about such matters. Balfour told the Cabinet of the

difficulties of the various Prime Ministers in their own Dominions, where there appeared to be a widespread, though erroneous, view that they were in some way subjected to the British government,

13

notwithstanding that the latter could not levy a penny in, raise a recruit in, or conclude a Treaty on behalf of, any Dominion. The task of the Committee had been to make the practice of the Constitution conform to the realities of the position.[1]

In law, the United Kingdom Parliament retained considerable authority over the Dominions. It had the technical right to legislate for them, as for the rest of the Empire. The Governor-General could withhold a Bill passed by a Dominion parliament from operation for a year. In South Africa, it was possible for the King – effectively, for the British Government – to disallow a law passed by the Dominion legislature. Such rights, reflected Balfour, were 'historical survivals which had long fallen into abeyance and which could not be revived without disastrous results'. The Committee over which Balfour presided offered a definition of 'Dominion status', later endorsed by the Imperial Conference. The Dominions, and the United Kingdom itself, were

> autonomous communities within the British Empire, equal in status, in no way subordinate to one another in any aspect of their domestic or external affairs, though united by a common allegiance to the Crown and freely associated as members of the British Commonwealth of Nations.

The word 'Commonwealth' was coming increasingly into use. At this time it was ambiguous, although a more exact definition was attempted many years later. Sometimes it was used as a synonym for 'Empire', more acceptable to people with 'progressive' opinions, and a conscience about past imperialism. Sometimes it was used in a more restricted sense to mean those countries that were already self-governing.

The formal link between the Dominions and Britain, and each other, was the Crown. 'Allegiance' was in one sense no more than a legal fiction, for it certainly did not imply any obligation to follow the known or believed wishes of the Sovereign. In another sense it had more substance, for in some at least of the Dominions there was a widespread affection for the King and a feeling that the British Empire was a kind of family, of which he was head. The Imperial Conference's assertion that the Dominions and the United Kingdom were 'in no way subordinate to one another' was important. Most of the Dominions derived their existing institutions, in law at least, from Acts of the United Kingdom Parliament. Some of these Acts reserved special powers to the United Kingdom. It seemed fair to interpret the new statement as meaning that the United Kingdom would henceforth defer to the Dominion Parliament in constitutional matters.

What the Imperial Conference said was, no doubt, a correct statement of principles and actual practice; but it had no legal authority, and such authority could be conferred only by an Act of Parliament. The process of drafting a Bill was not easy, and successive British Governments wrestled with a measure, which eventually became known as the Statute of Westminster, designed to define the relationship. This was essentially a verbal difficulty rather than a party-political problem, and the two changes of government which took place between the 1926 Conference and the final passage of the Statute of Westminster late in 1931 did not affect the general character of the measure they were attempting to enact.

The Act that was eventually passed did not repeat the Balfour Committee's definition of Dominion status; but there was a specific statement that an Act of a Dominion Parliament should not be held void because it conflicted with English law, or with an Act of the United Kingdom Parliament. It was also stated that no future Act of the United Kingdom Parliament should extend to a Dominion unless that Dominion so requested. Such a request might well be made, for example, when an old Act had set out the constitution of the Dominion, which the Dominion Parliament later wished to alter. Although the Statute of Westminster did not say so in as many words, it was generally taken that it would give any Dominion the right to leave the Empire should it so desire. Not long after the 1926 Conference, General Hertzog, Prime Minister of South Africa, asserted that this right existed, and nobody in authority contradicted him.

Most of the Dominions were unlikely to secede in the foreseeable future; but how did the Bill affect Ireland? The Irish Free State was, from its inception, in a very different position from the other Dominions. The other Dominions had been set up by British legislation which appeared to receive general approval in the country concerned. The Irish Free State had been established as an autonomous state as the result of an uneasy compromise which nobody really liked and which many Irishmen sought to overturn, if necessary by force. So would the Statute of Westminster give the Irish Free State the right to override the Treaty of 1921–22 which had defined relations between Britain and the Free State, and leave the Empire if she chose? In the parliamentary debates over the Bill, there were fierce altercations between Winston Churchill – currently out of office – who suspected that Ireland would act in that way, and Joseph Devlin, Nationalist MP for a Northern Ireland constituency, who indignantly denied the suggestion.[2] What Churchill said was later proved correct, but it was mischievous, and a high embarrassment to all who sought to set old quarrels aside. What Devlin said no doubt represented an honest statement of his own view; but he was in no position to commit the Irish Free State, and events proved him wrong. Most MPs of all parties probably preferred to believe that the problem did not exist.

Another important development, which was to affect the Empire as a whole, commenced soon after the Statute of Westminster received Royal approval, near the end of 1931. This matter also had deep roots. Before 1914, Britain had pursued a policy of free trade. When tariffs or other trade barriers existed at all, these were usually designed exclusively to raise revenue and did not distinguish between Imperial and non-Imperial trade. The same rule applied to those colonies whose trading policies were controlled from London. The self-governing parts of the Empire, and also India, often imposed tariffs on goods from external sources, including Britain; but this matter lay, for practical purposes, outside the control of the United Kingdom Parliament. From 1915 onwards, there were some qualifications of the Free Trade position in Britain itself; but until the 1930s it was broadly true to say that Britain did not interfere with the right of the peoples in her Empire to trade as they wished with foreign countries.

The 'Great Depression' which began in 1929 produced a profound effect on the trading policies of Britain and many other countries. There was a massive swing towards increased tariffs and other trade barriers. Trade restrictions generated international tensions, even between countries within the British Empire. Thus, at one point in 1931, there were sharp differences between Canada and New Zealand over tariff policies.

In August 1931, a National Government was set up in Britain. Originally it was a sort of three-party coalition (though the word 'coalition' was studiously avoided), but it soon became a predominantly Conservative administration, with a few hangers-on from other parties. Early in 1932, the National Government imposed a general system of tariffs on British imports. On most goods, the rate was 10 per cent *ad valorem*; but there were a number of special cases. Goods from the Empire were, for the time being, exempt. Later in the year, the Imperial Economic Conference at Ottawa resulted in a string of agreements affecting Britain, the Dominions, India and Southern Rhodesia, which, though a Colony, was permitted to negotiate independently. Exemption of Imperial goods would be continued, but the manner of assessment of tariffs on foreign imports would be changed. Furthermore, a considerable number of types of foreign goods (particularly certain foodstuffs), which had not been subjected to import duties under the earlier Acts, were to be dutiable, in order to give Imperial producers an advantage in British markets. In reciprocity, many British products were to be admitted into Empire markets either without duty or at a lower rate of duty than foreign goods.

Most of the colonies were not able to negotiate on their own behalf at Ottawa, but in the years that followed the Conference, Britain was able to exercise control over their trading policies. A famous example was the imposition of quotas on Japanese imports into Nigeria and the Gold Coast in 1934.[3] In those days, Japanese goods were notoriously cheap. Thus in one step the British Government contrived to put further burdens on the impoverished West African consumer, and to antagonise Japan.

Certainly the Empire was becoming increasingly important in Britain's overseas trade in the inter-war years – though there is room for debate as to how far this was due to the policies of Imperial governments, how far it was due to restrictive policies of foreign states and how far it was due to quite different causes. According to one author, in 1913 24.9 per cent of Britain's imports and 37.2 per cent of her exports represented trade with the British Empire, while by 1934 the respective figures were 35.3 per cent and 44.0 per cent.[4] Other authors give somewhat different figures for the relative growth of imperial trade,[5] but the overall picture is similar.

*

Important changes of a different kind were taking place about this time, which initially concerned particular countries in the Empire, although they would later have much wider repercussions. By the end of 1919, there was little doubt that India would eventually attain Dominion status, and it gradually became apparent that this would include the right to secede from the Empire if she so desired; but the way, and the speed, with which the change would take place were by no means apparent. The idea of *swaraj*, or Home Rule, continued to develop. The Indian National Congress had been established in the nineteenth century as a forum for Indian opinion, with British encouragement. After 1918, however, Congress rapidly became, for practical purposes, a political movement aiming at national independence, though this expression did not necessarily imply separation from the British Empire. Congress desired cooperation between Hindu and Muslim, but this cooperation rapidly broke down. Muslims had formed 10.9 per cent of Congress delegates in 1921; two years later they represented only 3.6 per cent.[6] Soon there were strong Muslim political organisations in India, which were deeply apprehensive of the likely consequences of *swaraj* for people of their own religion.

The place of Mohandas Gandhi in the story would be difficult to overstate. Gandhi, often known as Mahatma – 'great soul' – had received legal training in England, and later attracted considerable attention for his defence of the rights of Indians resident in South Africa. He had once been very sympathetic to British influence in India, but had swung strongly against it in the immediate aftermath of the war. He was moved at least as much by religious motives as political, and yet his religion would be difficult to define in familiar terms. By origin a Hindu, he was deeply influenced by ideas from other religions, particularly Christianity and Islam. There was a strong element of asceticism in his character, and his frail figure, clad only in a loincloth and sandals, was familiar world-wide – and a particular delight for cartoonists. His moral authority and influence over followers and admirers in India and elsewhere were enormous. On a number of occasions he undertook voluntary fasts to produce a political result. As he was obviously quite prepared to carry one of those fasts to death, the consequences of his fasting could be incalculable.

Gandhi's vision was of an independent and truly united India, within which Hindus and Muslims would cooperate freely, and the ancient stigma of an 'untouchable' caste would disappear. Gandhi looked to an India which would reject many of the values of the industrialised world in favour of a much simpler kind of life. The major instrument for achieving that objective would be non-violent resistance to an authority which was perceived as unjust. Gandhi's developing view that British policy was so morally flawed that Indians should not cooperate with existing authorities was soon adopted by Congress, though for mixed reasons. But early in 1922 an ugly and violent incident persuaded Gandhi to call off the campaign for non-cooperation, to the consternation of some of his own supporters. Soon afterwards, however, he was taken to prison by the British authorities for his pains. Released after two years, Gandhi dropped out of political activity for a while.

Not all Indian 'nationalists' were prepared to follow the peaceful policy which Gandhi recommended. There were occasional riots in many parts of India. In the twelve months from April 1926, for example, nearly 200 people were killed and eight times that number injured in various disturbances in different parts of India. These disturbances, however, had disparate causes,[7] and cannot all be regarded as aspects of a struggle designed to drive the British from India.

People in Britain watched the scene in India with bemusement. Some Britons were imperialists of the old school, determined to maintain power if this was physically possible, for the benefit of British rather than Indian interests. Others saw merits in the British Raj from India's point of view. They considered that British administration was a good deal more impartial in deciding disputes between Indians than any indigenous authority was likely to be, and was more efficient as well. There was real concern that, in a country where most people were illiterate, any speedy transfer of power to Indians would necessarily mean that a small educated élite would be set in unchallengeable control. Yet, whatever one might think about the merits of different kinds of government for India, events had acquired a momentum of their own, over which no individual or organisation, British or Indian, had full control.

A major new British initiative began in 1927. It had been agreed in 1919 that the reforms of that year would be reviewed ten years later; but the Conservative Government of Stanley Baldwin jumped the gun and set up what became known as the Statutory Commission on Indian Reforms. The thinking behind this decision appears to have been to some extent party-political, but there were also deeper considerations. At the time of the 1919 Act, the general view had been that the operation of 'dyarchy' in Provincial adminis-trations might be changed at decennial intervals, gradually reducing the number of topics which would be reserved for the Governors' nominees 'until in the fullness of time the transferred subjects com-prised the whole administration and "full responsible government" was thereby achieved'.[8]

The Chairman of the Statutory Commission was Sir John Simon, still a Liberal in those days; the other members were four Conservative and two Labour parliamentarians. Simon was a major figure in his party; the others were more or less unknown at the time, although they included Clement Attlee, who would one day become Labour Prime Minister. Lord Birkenhead, the Secretary of State for India, had originally contemplated including Indian members, but had later decided against this, considering that – if they were included – there would be no chance of a unanimous report emerging. He appears to have decided that, in the last analy-sis, it was more important to square British politicians than to satisfy Indians. The absence of Indian members excited immediate and adverse comment in India, but fears of serious boycotting were eventually stilled. The Commission sought, so far as possible, to gather information on the spot, and made a lengthy visit to India, which ended in April 1929.

When Labour took office a couple of months later, Government cooperation with the Viceroy of India, the Conservative Lord Irwin – the future Lord Halifax – continued. In order to reassure Indian opinion of British *bona fides* about future Indian constitutional development, Irwin soon announced that the goal of British policy was Dominion status for India. In one sense, this statement was no more than a reiteration of what had actually been promised at the time of the 1919 legislation, but it precipitated a furious debate over India, most particularly in the ranks of the Conservative Party. Winston Churchill, who had been Chancellor of the Exchequer in Baldwin's Government from 1924 to 1929, was most conspicuous of all the critics.

The effect of the debate was completely different from the wishes of any of the British politicians involved. Many Indians interpreted the public criticism of the line which was being supported by the three party leaders and Irwin alike, as the mark of a fundamental

British insincerity. At the end of 1929, Congress, meeting in Lahore, declared in favour of complete Indian independence and proclaimed a campaign of civil disobedience.

Almost at the same moment, the Great Depression began to have a serious impact on India. Export prices fell, there was a flight of capital and a currency crisis.[9] A declining economy promoted political discontent. Thus far, the debate over *swaraj* had been conducted overwhelmingly by middle-class people, who were feeling what one writer has described as 'collective frustration' in the aftermath of war.[10] Then, in the spring of 1930, Indian nationalists began to make a powerful appeal to the poor and dispossessed. Gandhi led a march in protest against the Indian government's salt tax: a gesture that attracted enormous publicity. The yield of the tax represented only a small proportion of the national revenue, but it fell particularly heavily on the poor, and unauthorised salt manufacture was forbidden. Gandhi defied the law and very publicly manufactured salt. He was arrested and imprisoned. This had a great effect on Indian views and action. In June 1930, a Cabinet Memorandum noted

> that among all classes of Indians there is a great and growing sense of national and racial consciousness which finds expression in opposition to foreign rule .... The overt movement has developed at a speed and with a momentum which has taken by surprise the most qualified observers, and this development has occurred since the Statutory Commission completed its labours in India.[11]

A wave of civil disobedience followed, which in many cases was accompanied by the violence of which Gandhi so earnestly disapproved. By the end of 1930, 54,000 people had been convicted of civil disobedience offences, of whom 23,000 remained in prison.

Meanwhile the Statutory Commission continued its slow labours, and in June 1930 the Report was published. The proposals fell short of a recommendation of immediate Dominion status, but went a considerable way in that direction. The Government took a new initiative and summoned a 'Round Table Conference', including representatives of the British parties and also of a wide range of Indian opinion. Congress, however, refused to participate. The Conference nevertheless soon declared in favour of Dominion status. When it closed in January 1931, the Prime Minister announced that the Government proposed gradually to extend the authority of provincial Indian legislatures. A couple of months later, Irwin – nearing the end of his period as Viceroy – released Gandhi from prison. The civil disobedience campaign ended, and so did the Ordinances with which the Government had been fighting it. Disorders in India abated considerably.

The alternation of good and bad relations with Congress, and most particularly with Gandhi, continued. Early in 1932 there was another spate of large-scale civil disobedience; but this gradually abated as the year advanced. The disturbances, however, were beginning to take on a social as well as a narrowly nationalist character. As the new Secretary of State for India, Sir Samuel Hoare told the Cabinet, 'The depressed classes constituted an entirely new problem. For the first time these classes were emerging as a conscious political force.'[12] Perhaps neither the British Cabinet nor most of the leaders of the Indian independence movement had yet taken full measure of the change which was taking place.

In the course of 1935, a new Government of India Act was passed. Burma was to be separated from India. Eleven autonomous Provinces were to be established, which would have directly elected Legislative Assemblies on a much wider franchise than before, though they still fell far short of universal suffrage. The old system of dyarchy, under which some Departments of State were responsible to Provincial Councils while others reported directly to the Governors, would end, and the Governors were to be advised by ministers responsible to the legislatures, except on a few reserved matters, which included the interests of minorities. A Federal legislature for the whole of India would be set up when adequate support had been received from the Princely States. It would have control over matters of general importance, including currency and tariffs. Defence, foreign relations and religious affairs would remain the responsibility of the Viceroy.

Congress views on whether to participate in the working of the Act were divided. A substantial element, headed by the avowed republican and socialist Jawaharlal (Pandit) Nehru, favoured boycott, but they were defeated by nearly a two to one majority in their own organisations and Congress resolved to participate. One suspects that local Congress leaders found the idea of becoming members of their Provincial legislatures an attractive one. In the first elections under the new Constitution, Congress won 45 per cent of the seats, securing absolute control of five out of eleven Provinces, and running a little short of a majority in a sixth. Eventually, Congress came to control eight Provincial governments. The later 1930s proved a much more peaceful period in India than the early part of the decade had been.

*

Developments in India were bound to have repercussions in many other places. Southern Ireland had only about 1 per cent of the population of India, yet its problems probably rank second in importance to those of India for the future of the Empire as a whole.

The rôle of Éamon de Valera was to prove almost as critical for Ireland as that of Gandhi was for India. An important figure in the 1916 rising, he was sentenced to death in the aftermath, but escaped execution through a technicality. After many of his friends had been executed, and de Valera came so close to death himself, he could hardly take a dispassionate view of relations between his own country and Britain. He had opposed the Anglo-Irish Treaty during debates in the Dáil, and gave public support to the Republicans during the civil war which followed a few months later. De Valera never made any secret of his wish to establish Ireland as a Republic outside the British Empire, but he eventually came to the view that the republican status which he desired might well be established gradually, not by a single traumatic act of separation. De Valera excluded himself from the Dáil for several years, but he returned in 1927. The republican party with which he was associated, Fianna Fáil, was able to form a Government in February 1932, and de Valera was to hold the chief executive office in Ireland until 1948.

The new Government was involved in dispute with Britain on several scores. Most immediately serious of these was the Free State's decision to abolish payment to Britain under the various Land Purchase Acts. These Acts, which had been passed in the late nineteenth and early twentieth centuries, had empowered the British Government to buy out Irish landlords and transfer their land to peasants, who would repay the money under what amounted to very long-term mortgages. Under the Treaty of 1921–22, the Irish

Free State Government undertook to continue repayments. Many of these loans were still outstanding in the 1930s.

The decision to abolish the Land Purchase payments stirred deep emotions in both countries. In Ireland, landlords had long been regarded as a particularly oppressive feature of British rule. In Britain, however, the Irish action was widely seen as an inexcusable act of bad faith. The British Government retorted by imposing special import duties on goods from the Irish Free State. These duties were designed to produce sufficient revenue to compensate for loss of payment under the Land Purchase Acts. The proceeds were not adequate for the purpose, and the duties were later increased. Not surprisingly, this 'trade war' proved damaging to the economies of both countries. Irish agricultural exports suffered; so also did British exports of coal, which had previously been sent to Ireland in exchange.

The Irish Free State also took action to reduce its Imperial links. The oath of allegiance to the King which had been taken by members of the Dáil was abolished. The office of Governor-General was first reduced to a sinecure, then abolished. When Edward VIII was about to abdicate the British throne in December 1936, the first reaction of the Free State Government was to express total indifference. It was then pointed out that, unless action was taken in Dublin, Edward would remain, in law, King of Ireland. The point was accepted; the Dáil promptly removed all reference to the King, save in matters concerning external relations, from the Free State's constitution.[13] In 1937 a new Constitution was adopted for the country, which became known as Éire.

The final move of the inter-war period was of a more friendly character. In 1938, a general agreement was reached between the British and Éireann Governments. Naval bases in southern Ireland, which had been reserved for Britain under the 1921–22 Treaty, were ceded to Éire, and British claims for special facilities for military and naval forces were renounced. The trade war was ended; an agreed sum of £10 million was paid by the Éire Government in settlement of the wrangle over land annuities.

Technically, Éire was still not a Republic; but it was one for most practical purposes, and nobody would be likely to raise such serious objection when and if the final step was taken. The significance of these complex events was very wide indeed. A signal had been sent to the whole British Empire that any self-governing Dominion was not only free to leave the Empire in a legal sense, but could actually do so without disaster supervening. Other Dominions might take a very different view about the desirability of retaining imperial links; but they had a real choice in the matter.

Inter-war events in South Africa were also important for the future both of that country and of others. The black majority was largely disenfranchised, but in the early 1920s, two large parties of white people operated in the Union. Each was led by a famous Boer General of the 1899–1902 war: the South African Party by Jan Smuts, and the Nationalist Party by J.B.M. Hertzog. In 1932–33, however, the two large parties decided to fuse, forming the United Party. This left some extreme republican and ultra-racist Nationalists in the cold. A new movement, the *Gesuiwerdes*, or 'Purified Nationalists', emerged, headed by Dr D.F. Malan. They formed a group of between 20 and 30 MPs, while the United Party had well over 100, and there were various small parties. Tiny though they were, the 'Purified Nationalists' became the recognised opposition and thus could reasonably hope that some turn of events would occur sooner or later, which would give them great influence and perhaps overall power.

One Dominion underwent experiences of a profoundly different nature which also illustrated the very plastic nature of Imperial institutions. As in several other parts of the Empire, important events in Newfoundland were sparked off by the Great Depression. Newfoundland, which was sometimes described as 'the oldest colony', had been first settled by the British in the sixteenth century. In the nineteenth century it received the opportunity to join Canada, but chose not to do so. When the general concept of 'Dominion status' developed, Newfoundland ranked as a separate Dominion, though it had a much smaller population than any of the others – well under 300,000 people, of whom more than half belonged to families dependent on fisheries.

Towards the end of 1931, it became clear that the Government of Newfoundland was insolvent and could not service its public debt. As an emergency measure, half of the required sum was defrayed by Newfoundland, the remainder being provided as a loan by Britain and Canada.[14] Various long-term solutions to the problem were suggested, but were ruled out for various reasons. Eventually, in November 1933, agreement was reached between the United Kingdom, Canada and Newfoundland. The existing form of government would be suspended until the island was self-supporting. A Commission of Government would be set up, presided over by the Governor, with three representatives each from the United Kingdom and Newfoundland. The departments of government would be divided between the six Commissioners. In the meantime, the United Kingdom would assume responsibility for the island's finances. This strange state of affairs was to endure for a very long time, and was not finally resolved until Newfoundland decided to join Canada in 1949.

*

During the inter-war period, there was a major shift in policy of British Governments towards the Colonial dependencies. It is difficult to point to any particular event which marked the change; but in 1942 – not long after Churchill's 'liquidation' speech – the Colonial Secretary, Viscount Cranborne, made an authoritative statement of current attitudes. This statement was made with evident concern to allay American suspicions of continuing British 'imperialism', but appears to be a fair account of an attitude which had already existed for a number of years. Cranborne declared that 'the ultimate objective of our policy has been and is to promote self-government in the Colonies'.[15]

He went on to add that 'many of the peoples of the British Colonial Empire are not yet ready for full self-government, and will not be ready for some considerable time', and expressed doubt whether premature grant of self-government 'would be for the happiness and prosperity of the people themselves'. Cranborne contemplated that the British link would continue; that erstwhile colonies would follow the precedent of the Dominions, and play 'an ever-increasing part in the British Commonwealth of free nations'.

By the outbreak of war in 1939, it was clear that the British Empire was bound to become a much looser association than in the past. The recent record, particularly in India, suggested that the change would be peaceful, and there seemed a fair chance that the members, with the exception of Éire, would elect to continue many of their links with Britain. All this, however, was predicated on the assumption that imperial development was able to proceed in an organic manner, without any violent interruption from external events.

3
Coming of War

Many people described the 1914 war as an 'imperialist war'. Whatever might be said of the 1939 conflict, it was nothing of the kind – from Britain's point of view at least. By 1937, there were already many signs which suggested that a major war was likely in the near future. Early in the year, the Chiefs of Staff Sub-committee of the Committee of Imperial Defence provided a review of the military situation, which was circulated to the Cabinet.[1] As they put it:

> Neither aggression nor expansion forms any part in British policy, and, consequently, security is only likely to be threatened through an expansionist policy on the part of some other Powers.

Evidently Britain had no further imperial ambitions of her own. Furthermore,

> The available evidence does not show that any Power intends a direct act of aggression against the British Empire in the immediate future.

So what risks existed? The chief danger, the Chiefs of Staff decided, was that Britain might become involved in war with Germany, Japan and Italy simultaneously. A year later, they were very blunt indeed about the consequences which would arise in that event. They left the Government in no doubt that if France was Britain's only major ally in such a war, defeat was probable.[2]

But if the British Empire neither coveted territory from others, nor was directly threatened by anybody else, then how could such a perilous situation arise? In the origin of the 1914 war, political ideology as such had played little part. In the late 1930s, however, matters were completely different. A great many people, in Britain and elsewhere, were coming to see international problems as a world-wide struggle between the forces of 'Dictatorship' and the forces of 'Democracy'. Long before war came in 1939, such people were anticipating – even desiring – a final reckoning between the conflicting ideologies; and this concern completely overrode any real interest in Imperial defence. This outlook influenced many supporters and opponents of the government alike, and increasing pressure was put upon it to resist 'Dictatorship' and, in particular, any territorial aspirations which 'Dictators' might have, whether or not they cut across Britain's own obvious interests.

The international controversies into which Britain was being drawn in the inter-war period contrasted sharply with those of the early twentieth century not only in the large 'ideological' element present, but also in the extent to which Britain was responding to events and policies which were in no sense of her own making. In 1902, she had made a treaty of alliance with Japan, which was visibly related to imperial interests. In the early 1920s, pressure from the United States compelled her to abrogate that treaty.[3] Thus Britain lost her special influence with Japan, and was unable to restrain Japan's increasingly aggressive policy in the 1930s. On the other side of the world, Britain's concern with the defence of France involved her in the affairs of eastern Europe. In the area between, commitment to the League of Nations brought Britain into deep dispute with Italy. Such policies had nothing to do with defence of the British Empire: indeed, they diverted an enormous amount of effort away from imperial defence.

To this one might add that it was never very clear where Britain should organise her system of defence. If she contemplated war in defence of parts of the British Empire, one system of defence preparations was appropriate; if she contemplated a war in Europe, or a war in defence of the principles of the League of Nations, a completely different system of preparations was required.

In 1937, there had been many expressions of pride in the British Empire, particularly in connection with the coronation of George VI and the Imperial Conference; and yet British public interest in the existing problems of Empire was minimal. Among people of all political views, the principal concern was with Britain's own internal problems, followed by concern for the politics of western and central Europe, with the Empire a very poor third indeed. On a rough count, the House of Commons Hansard for the 1936–37 Session gives 300 references to India – surely Britain's chief source of imperial anxiety – and 1,000 to Spain: a fair sample of where the concerns of MPs and their constituents lay. Yet India, unlike Spain, was a direct British responsibility, with perhaps fifteen times the population.

The part played by the Empire, and particularly by the Dominions in the run-up to the 1939 conflict, was very different in some ways from what it had been in 1914. In the earlier war, the doctrine of 'unity of the Crown' prescribed that the King could not simultaneously be at war and at peace. If, therefore, war was declared by Britain, all other parts of the Empire were automatically involved. In the late 1930s, it was widely assumed that the self-governing Dominions would need to make their own individual declarations of war.

During the 'Munich' crisis of September 1938, there were several anxious meetings between the High Commissioners for the Dominions and Malcolm MacDonald[4] – Dominions Secretary and son of the former Prime Minister Ramsay MacDonald. The picture which soon emerged was that, if Britain went to war, Australia, New Zealand and Canada would do the same. But Éire, which was still treated as a Dominion for the purpose of these meetings, would seek to remain neutral, although 'geographical circumstances were such that Éire might well become involved before long'.

There was much doubt about South Africa. The Dominion's High Commissioner explained that his Government 'would use all their endeavours to persuade the United Kingdom not to enter war in defence of France unless and until it was clear that France was in danger of being overwhelmed, which would be regarded as involving a threat to Great Britain'.[5] The Prime Minister General Hertzog was even more blunt, and 'made it clear on more than one occasion to H.M. Government that South Africa cannot be expected to take any part in a war over Czechoslovakia'.[6]

The 'Munich' settlement which emerged at the end of September 1938 was generally approved in the Dominions, even though a substantial section of British opinion was deeply critical. Lord Tweedsmuir, Governor-General of Canada, wrote to Prime Minister Chamberlain, strongly condemning the 'fatuous criticism of your policy in the British press'.[7] This he contrasted with its Canadian counterparts, which had mostly been 'wonderful'.

A year later, events in the even graver crisis over Poland moved too swiftly for Dominion opinion to be clearly formulated. Germany attacked Poland on 1 September 1939; Britain declared war two days later. Robert Menzies, Prime Minister of Australia, promptly announced that 'Great Britain has declared war, and ... as a result Australia is also at war'. This sounded very much like the old 'unity of the Crown' doctrine. New Zealand delayed a few hours, while the Prime Minister consulted his Cabinet colleagues.[8] Both countries decided to issue their own separate declarations of war on the same day as Britain. Canada's support was immediately promised by Prime Minister Mackenzie King and by the Opposition. But as recently as the Imperial Conference of 1937, the Canadian representative had made it plain that there were several very different schools of thought about the defence of his country.[9] Perhaps for this reason it was decided to await the meeting of the Canadian Parliament. On 10 September, an Address which was, in effect, a declaration of war was adopted by the Canadian House of Commons without a division – the few doubters deciding not to force a vote. It was then endorsed unanimously by the Senate. The slight delay, and the decision to leave the matter to the Canadian Parliament, was an intimation that Canada was more anxious than the Pacific Dominions to assert that the choice ultimately lay in her own hands, not in those of Britain.

In South Africa, matters were on a knife-edge. The United Party had a huge overall majority; but its Cabinet was almost evenly divided on the issue of declaring war. Prime Minister Hertzog favoured neutrality; his Deputy Smuts took the other view. The division between their respective supporters followed roughly the lines of the groups which had formed the United Party a few years earlier. Those who had belonged to the old Nationalist Party mostly favoured neutrality; the old South African Party favoured belligerence. The neutralists were supported by the 'Purified Nationalists' who followed Malan. Two smaller parties favoured intervention. On 6 September, the South African Parliament decided, by 80 votes to 67, to go to war. Hertzog sought a dissolution of Parliament from the Governor-General. This was refused: a remarkable decision, surely, from a constitutional viewpoint. Hertzog resigned and Smuts became Prime Minister: an office he was to hold for nine years.

The far from overwhelming majority in favour of South Africa's declaration of war was followed by developments of a disturbing character. Hertzog soon withdrew from politics, though not before he had delivered himself of the astonishing opinion that a National Socialist system was appropriate for South Africa. Leadership of the Nationalists eventually passed to Malan. But when the views of the South African electors were sought, at the General Election of 1943, the response was a comfortable win for Smuts.

In Éire, the Dáil resolved to remain neutral. Neville Chamberlain recognised the inevitability of that decision, telling the British Cabinet that he 'did not doubt the truth of Mr de Valera's assertion that the creed of Ireland was neutrality and that no government could exist that departed from that principle'.[10] This was by no means the end of the matter. Winston Churchill, who had recently joined the Cabinet, was deeply exercised about the 'Treaty Ports' Queenstown (now Cóbh), Berehaven and Lough Swilly. Britain had retained control of these three ports under the Anglo-Irish Treaty of 1921, but they had been relinquished to Éire under the arrangements of 1938. Five weeks into the war, there was a deep discussion in Cabinet, where the three questions of Éire's constitutional position in relation to the Empire, her right to remain neutral and possible action over the 'Treaty Ports' were bound together.[11] 'What is the international juridical status of Southern Ireland?' Churchill had demanded in a letter written to the Foreign Secretary shortly before.[12] 'It is not a Dominion. They themselves repudiate the idea. It is certainly under the Crown. Nothing has been defined.'

Whatever might be Éire's status, was she entitled to be neutral? Anthony Eden, who had returned to office at the same time as Churchill, and was now Dominions Secretary, gave a practical, rather than a legal, answer:

> We could, no doubt, challenge Éire's neutrality on legal grounds. But if we adopted that course we should not have the support of Canada or South Africa. Both those Dominions have taken the

view that they were entitled to decide whether, if this country declared war, they should declare war also. Even if we could prove that Éire was not entitled to remain neutral and at the same time to remain a member of the British Commonwealth, the result would be ... that Éire would cease to be a member of the British Commonwealth.[13]

At the same Cabinet meeting, Churchill hinted at the possibility that action might be taken to reclaim the 'Treaty Ports'. Chamberlain gave an answer which – at least for the time being – was convincing: 'Seizure of the ports ... would have the most unfortunate repercussions in the United States and in India.' The Prime Minister might have added that any military action against Éire would create immense security problems in Northern Ireland and, indeed, in all parts of the Commonwealth where there had been substantial Irish immigration. In 1943, and again in 1944, there would be General Elections in Éire. Both resulted in victories for de Valera's Fianna Fáil; but even more significant was the fact that neutrality was not an issue between the Irish parties on either occasion. On that matter at least de Valera evidently spoke for his country as a whole.

Although the doctrine of unity of the Crown had lapsed so far as the Dominions were concerned, it still applied to the Colonies, and the British declaration of war automatically brought them into the conflict. There was little sign of protest in the colonial Empire, either from native peoples or from settlers. In India, too, the doctrine of unity of the Crown still applied. When Britain went to war, the Viceroy, Lord Linlithgow, made a brief broadcast statement informing the country that it was also at war. The manner of India's involvement soon stirred up a great hornets' nest, but the main complaint did not come, as in South Africa, from people who opposed the war. There were some Indians who took that view; but far more numerous were people who wished to link the war with internal Indian problems.

India was in a most curious constitutional condition in September 1939, and Indian reactions to the war may best be understood in the context of recent political developments. Although Congress controlled eight of the eleven Provinces of 'British India', the Indian Federation which Britain had proposed to set up under the Government of India Act of 1935 was not yet in existence, and fundamental questions concerning the powers of such a Federation were in deep dispute at the outbreak of war. Different Indians objected to the current Federation plans for very different reasons. Congress contended that the powers proposed for the centre were inadequate: specifically, it demanded that the 'reserved' subjects of external affairs, defence and finance should be removed from British control and passed to the Federation. There were also objections to existing plans for representation of the Princely States within the Federation.

The Princely States posed problems of their own. The Government of India Act of 1935 prescribed that the Federation should not come into being until enough Princely States had acceded to fill half of their representation in the Upper House of the legislature, and to represent half the total population of the States. On the eve of war Lord Zetland, Secretary of State for India, was still trying to persuade reluctant Princes to give the necessary support.[14] Even more serious were the apprehensions of the Muslim League, which was disturbed about the proposed Federation for reasons almost diametrically opposed to those of Congress. The Muslim League feared a strong central authority because it would necessarily be under Hindu domination. Some Muslims were moving towards the idea of introducing another tier of government, a Confederation of the Muslim provinces, before the Federation was set up.

Both Congress and the Muslim League were playing for political credibility. Congress wished to be regarded as the authentic voice which spoke for all Indians, whatever their religion. Early in 1940, it even went to the point of choosing one of the relatively few remaining Muslim adherents as its President. In practice, the overwhelming majority of politically active Muslims, and many Hindus as well, dissented passionately from Congress claims to speak for India as a whole. The Muslim League sought to represent itself as the voice of all Indian Muslims: another profound inaccuracy. Most Indians of all religions had no vote, and their political views – if any – were unknown.

Three weeks into the war, the Secretary of State for India circulated the Cabinet with a Memorandum in which he declared that there was 'little doubt that the general trend of public opinion in India was in full sympathy with the Allied aims'.[15] Gandhi evidently concurred, telling the Viceroy 'that he viewed the war "with an

English heart" and would personally favour unconditional support for the Allies'.[16] Nehru's attitude appeared similar. But major difficulties had already arisen, even before the Cabinet Memorandum had been issued. On 15 September, Congress demanded a statement of British war aims in their application to India, with the implication that unless this produced a satisfactory response, Indian cooperation in the war would be withheld. What Congress further required was 'a declaration to the effect that India was an independent nation which was entitled to determine its own constitution by means of a Constituent Assembly, without any outside interference'.[17]

No belligerent Government ever likes to be pressed to state its war aims in any but the vaguest terms, for by so doing it is almost bound to alienate some of the people who had been supporting its prosecution of the war. In the present case, any declaration of war aims which would please Congress was sure to be viewed with dismay by the Muslim League and by the Princes, both of which groups had, on the whole, been supporting the British cause. The last thing the Viceroy wanted was to alienate anybody, and he had discussions with no fewer than 52 Indians prominent in political life. He encountered what were described, with commendable understatement, as 'marked differences'. At last, on 17 October, Linlithgow made a public statement which reiterated the familiar promise of eventual Dominion status; but the general contents of the Viceroy's statement were declared by the Congress Working Committee five days later to be 'wholly unsatisfactory'. The Muslim League, by contrast, was delighted.

Congress further called on the Party's Provincial Assemblies to withdraw cooperation with the Government and, on 1 November, the Congress Ministers resigned. Following procedures set out in the 1935 Act, the Governors took charge of Provincial administration of seven of the Provinces. In the eighth, Assam, it proved possible to set up a stable coalition without Congress. These stopgap arrangements proved tolerably successful. Congress was still in no mood to sabotage the official war effort; but it was also in no mood to give much positive assistance. So the British authorities were able to proceed with recruitment and other warlike measures with efficiency, but with little enthusiasm from leading politicians.

What had changed the attitude of Congress? The general view of the British Cabinet was that 'The left wing of Congress was out for trouble. The right wing was inclined to compromise with us, but could not carry its view. In order to preserve a united front it was identifying itself in public with the left wing.'[18] The one thing which no political leader ever, anywhere, can admit is that he does not have control over his own followers. Nevertheless, the general situation in India was still described as 'peaceful' at the end of 1939.[19]

At this point, new difficulties began to appear. The Muslim League called for a 'day of rejoicing' over the disappearance of the Congress ministries: an action which Congress could hardly fail to regard as provocative. In the spring of 1940, the Muslim League went a great deal further, and for the first time demanded partition of India into Muslim and non-Muslim areas. Here was the root of the idea of a separate 'Pakistan'.[20]

Not long after this, Chamberlain's administration was replaced by Winston Churchill's all-Party Coalition Government. A few weeks on came the fall of France. Britain's position was now desperate, and the new Government anxiously canvassed Indian support. In August 1940, the British Government formally proposed that India should attain Dominion status after the war, under a constitution framed by Indians themselves, subject to the protection of ethnic and social minorities, and the fulfilment of Treaty obligations to the Princely States.

The leading Congress personalities were by no means mollified and the position deteriorated rapidly. Nehru – who had taken quite a sympathetic attitude to Britain's cause at the beginning of the war – was arrested for making speeches which were 'not only anti-war but calculated to stir up agrarian discontent'.[21] Which was regarded as the greater offence is not clear. The Viceroy began to panic, anticipating that it would soon be necessary 'to proclaim Congress' – that is, to declare it an illegal organisation – and to 'arrest Working Committee, including Gandhi, and leaders of Congress in all Provinces'.[22] This suggestion was seen by the British Cabinet to be an over-reaction, and was firmly rejected.[23]

Two parts of the Empire came under enemy control in 1940. Soon after Germany seized northern and western France, the Channel Islands were also occupied and remained so until the Allies re-established themselves in Western Europe in 1944. British

Somaliland was abandoned to the Italians in August. The Italian occupation was brief, however, and the territory was restored to British control in the following year. In general, however, the British Empire was able to resist threats from Germany or Italy, largely because of the continuing strength of the British Navy. Thus the Mediterranean colonies of Gibraltar, Malta and Cyprus, and the mandated territory of Palestine, were all successfully protected, though Malta suffered savage bombardment.

The run-up to the 1939 war, and the first period of that war, had brought out clearly that the fault-lines which had been revealed in the earlier conflict still existed. Ireland, South Africa and India were, from the British Government's point of view, the major trouble-spots. The remaining Dominions, and the Colonies, had given much positive support to the British Government. It is fair to ask whether they were truly convinced about the merits of British policy, or whether they had acceded because a mixture of considerations – economic, military and sentimental – had disposed them to follow any British lead unless there were overwhelming reasons for refusing. Down to 1941, however, there was little sign that British 'official' opinion anticipated any major disruption in relations with the bulk of the Empire, except in the event of total defeat. To what extent that view was justified would soon become apparent.

4
The Impact of Japan

In April 1933, Sir Maurice Hankey, the extremely able and influential Secretary to the Cabinet, sent a warning to the Prime Minister:

> if ... we lost Singapore ... there would be a calamity of the first magnitude. We might well lose India and the faith in us of Australia and New Zealand would be shattered. The disaster to our trade would be overwhelming.[1]

The only country which could possibly offer a threat to Singapore at the time when Hankey wrote was Japan, which had attacked Manchuria a year and a half earlier. Singapore was later fortified; though – as events would later prove – in a woefully inadequate manner.

In the early twentieth century, Anglo-Japanese relations had been exceptionally good, and in 1902 Britain made her first departure from the traditional policy of 'splendid isolation' by concluding a Treaty with Japan. But when she abrogated that Treaty in the 1920s, she was compelled to face an increasingly hostile Japan.

With a very large and very vulnerable Empire in the Far East, Britain had every reason to keep Japan neutral when she went to war with Germany in 1939. But the United States was hostile to Japan, and Britain fell in with American policy, no doubt hoping desperately to win favour in Washington which might be of help against Germany. In the course of 1941, the two countries were able to exert such powerful economic pressure on Japan that she was virtually excluded from purchasing her vital requirements from South-East Asia. Japan was thus compelled either to capitulate to Anglo-American pressure or else to attack European and American possessions, in order to take by force what she was unable to secure through trade.

In December 1941, Japan attacked and destroyed a large part of the American Pacific Fleet at Pearl Harbor, and almost immediately invaded British and Dutch possessions in the Far East. Two great British naval vessels were rushed to the area, but they too were sunk. With command of the sea and strong land forces, the Japanese cut rapidly through Allied possessions. By the middle of 1942, they had overrun Malaya, Burma, Hong Kong and the northern part of Borneo, as well as the Netherlands East Indies (now Indonesia), the Philippines (then an American possession) and many other islands in the Pacific. In the south, they were close to Australia, in the west they were at the gates of India, in the east they were sufficiently close to the United States to render Japanese immigrants in California a perceived security risk. At this point the Japanese advance was halted. Very gradually, and at great cost in life, the Allies were able to retake some of the territories which had been seized; but even at the moment of Japanese capitulation in August 1945, a large part of the area was still in enemy hands.

The Japanese conquest of Malaya occupied only ten weeks in 1941–42. Defence was offered mainly by British, Australian and Indian troops, with residents in the peninsula playing only a small part. The episode ended with the surrender of the immensely important naval base of Singapore on 15 February 1942, in circumstances which are still a matter of deep controversy. When the conquest was complete, the northern part of Malaya was given to Japan's ally Thailand. The remainder was occupied by Japan herself, in conditions which led to great suffering and to bitter anti-Japanese feeling which persisted for years afterwards.

In Burma, the story was in some ways similar, in others very different. When the country was separated from India by the legislation of 1935, Burma became a colony, but received a large measure of internal autonomy, a rather wide franchise and an administration that was almost entirely Burmese. As in India, there was a strong demand for Dominion status in the early part of the war, and the Prime Minister, U Saw, visited London in the latter part of 1941 to seek support for that demand. During his progress homewards, the Japanese war broke out. The British authorities decided that there was evidence that U Saw had been in contact with the Japanese and he was interned in Africa for the remainder of the war.

The Japanese conquest of Burma was swift, though considerably more protracted than with Malaya. Rangoon fell in March 1942, Mandalay a couple of months later. By the middle of May, the country was more or less completely occupied. In contrast with the largely passive attitudes in Malaya, the Japanese had received substantial assistance from Burmese rebels. The insurgent leader was Aung San, who had spent time in Japan before returning to Burma early in 1941. He soon organised a group of young men, who became known as the 'Thirty Comrades'. During the Japanese attack, they were able to attract considerable numbers of recruits to support the invaders. In August 1942, the Japanese were able to establish a satellite 'government' in Burma under Dr Ba Maw, who in 1937 had become the first Burmese Prime Minister. A year later, the new 'government' formally declared the country's independence. Other important Burmese politicians took a very different view of events and fled to India, where a sort of 'government-in-exile' was established on the Allied side.

Other British territories in the path of the Japanese attack had different experiences again. As far back as January 1941, Churchill had told the Commander-in-Chief in the Far East that 'if Japan goes to war with us there is not the slightest chance of holding Hong Kong or relieving it'.[2] Some reinforcements were nevertheless sent there not long before the Japanese attack; but by the end of December 1941 the colony had capitulated. Japanese occupation of British possessions in the north of Borneo was also inevitable and swiftly achieved.

*

As the Japanese advanced through Burma, India was menaced as well, and so it became a matter of high importance for the Imperial authority to ensure that Indian sympathy was firmly on the British side. Was it possible to secure that result by some approach to the Indian political leaders? At first, Churchill was highly sceptical,[3] but as time went on and the military situation became increasingly grave, the Prime Minister and his colleagues began to waver. On 5 February 1942, the War Cabinet was confronted with two weighty memoranda, expressing very different views of how the matter should be handled. The Secretary of State for India, L.S. Amery, supported by the Viceroy, argued that no further constitutional advance could be made at that juncture without aggravating internal discords. Sir Stafford Cripps, a prominent member of the Labour Party, proposed that a renewed effort should be made to get the Indian political leaders to unite in active support of the war effort, and urged that a representative of the Government should be sent to India.[4] Perhaps more in despair than hope, the Cabinet accepted Cripps's view.

After much further discussion, it was agreed that Cripps should himself be sent to India, armed with a specific scheme, devised with the Cabinet's authority.[5] Immediately after the war, so the proposal ran, an elected Indian body should be charged with devising a new Constitution for India. The British Government undertook to accept and implement such a Constitution, subject to a few qualifications, most important of which was the right of any Province which was not prepared to accept the constitution to retain its existing status. This was not wildly different from what had been said a year and a half earlier, except that it gave a time limit and made rather more explicit the right of recalcitrant Provinces to contract out of the eventual deal. The Cabinet probably hoped that Cripps, who had close personal relations with many Indian leaders, might be able to exert influence where others had failed. Cripps reached India on 22 March, and the Government's proposals were published eight days later.

Whether the 'Cripps mission' would have had much chance of success in any circumstances is doubtful. Coinciding as it did with a period of very rapid Japanese advance, which carried with it the immediate prospect of a Japanese invasion of India, the 'mission' was more or less foredoomed. Why should the Indians follow a course of action which more or less committed them to the Allied side, when it looked as if the Allies might soon be defeated and Indians might need to negotiate with the victorious Japanese? Congress, the Muslim League and the Sikhs all rejected the British proposals, though for very disparate reasons. After the failure of the Cripps mission, Congress launched a major 'Quit India' campaign, which in some places was accompanied by serious violence. Many leaders of Congress were soon arrested. But nobody could have had much doubt that, whatever might happen, British imperial rule in India was close to its end.

In 1943, the Indian Government was confronted with a different kind of crisis, of enormous dimensions. Before the Japanese war, India had normally been self-supporting for food, save for 1.5 million tons of rice imported annually from Burma. In 1941–42 crops were below average, and Burmese supplies were cut off.[6] Early in August 1943, the British Cabinet was faced with an urgent request from the Government of India for half a million tons of wheat during the ensuing autumn and winter. The British agreed to send just 100,000 tons of barley from Iraq to India, and half that quantity of wheat from Australia to Ceylon, there to await instructions. Linlithgow was shocked at the paucity of this response:

> I am bound in terms to warn the Cabinet that the Government of India and I cannot be responsible for the continuing stability of India now, or for her capacity to serve as a base against Japan next year, unless we have appropriate help in prospect.[6]

Linlithgow was almost at the end of his Viceroyalty, but his chosen successor Lord Wavell took up the cause, and so did the Chiefs of Staff and the Secretary of State for India. Amery reported that famine conditions were already developing in industrial areas, particularly in Bengal, and pleaded with the Cabinet for the half million tons of grain originally demanded. This request was based on military as well as humanitarian grounds; but in the end only another 50,000 tons was provided, making in all just 40 per cent of the quantity for which the Indian authorities pleaded so earnestly.[7] The new Viceroy did what lay in his power to relieve the situation, using the army actively in food distribution and imposing statutory price controls and rationing. As with famines elsewhere, it is difficult to be sure how much mortality was directly attributable to starvation; but figures published by the Famine Inquiry Commission in 1945 indicated that one and a half million people died in Bengal in 1943–44 as a result of the famine and the epidemics that followed it.

In India, as in Burma, there were some nationalists who adhered actively to the enemy of the Imperial Power. Subhas Bose[8] had been a leading figure in the Indian National Congress for several years before the war. In 1938, he had been elected President of Congress with Gandhi's support; in the following year he was again elected President, but against Gandhi's opposition, and he was forced out a few months later. Before 1939, Bose had been disposed to support warlike nationalist demonstrations in India, and he apparently saw himself as a future dictator who would cut the Gordian knot of communal differences. During the Indian disturbances of the early part of the war, Bose was arrested and then went on hunger strike. His imprisonment was promptly switched to house arrest, from which he contrived to escape early in 1941. After an astonishing journey via Afghanistan he arrived in Germany, and was later transferred by submarine to Japan, where he landed in June 1943.

By this time, the nucleus of an 'Indian National Army' (INA) had been recruited to fight for Indian 'independence' alongside the Axis Powers. It drew largely on Indian prisoners-of-war from various battlefronts. Thus, when Singapore capitulated to the Japanese, 85,000 troops were captured, of whom nearly 60,000 were Indians; 25,000 of those Indians eventually joined the INA, no doubt for many different reasons. Later in 1943, the Japanese recognised a 'Provisional Indian Government' set up in Burma. Bose, who was put in charge, evidently contemplated that the INA and the 'Provisional Indian Government' would play an active rôle in driving the British out of India; but this was never put to the test. Bose himself died as the result of an aeroplane accident in 1945.

In the course of 1944, the immediate military threat to India was removed, and in that sense Indian constitutional questions became less urgent. The Viceroy was nevertheless anxious to produce a long-term solution if this was at all possible. Wavell sought British Cabinet authority to replace the existing Executive Council with a new body, which would be selected as a result of discussions with leaders of the Indian political parties. The Cabinet at first decided to refuse this request, but was deeply divided as to what – if anything – might be done. The Prime Minister's own views, as recorded in the Cabinet Minutes, are revealing:

If the Hindus, Moslems and other communities were prepared to accept the Cripps offer, he would be quite ready to see the Army withdrawn and India given full Dominion status. It would, indeed, from the military point of view, be a help to be relieved of our share in her defence.[9]

Behind these careful words seems to run the message that Churchill, for many years the arch-enemy of Indian independence, was now eager to accept any arrangement on which the Indians might agree – not only in order to please Indian opinion, but also in order to get Britain off a military hook. He was well aware that Dominion status included the right to secede altogether from the Empire, and that many Indians sought to vindicate this right.

For a time, Wavell appeared to be getting his way. A White Paper was published in June 1945, proposing that the Viceroy should set up an Executive Council chosen from leaders of Indian opinion with a sprinkling of other members with special experience. This, of course, was no more than a temporary expedient; but, if it worked, it might well point the way to a durable settlement. Preliminary meetings were promptly held in Simla. At first, there was considerable optimism. Towards the end of June, however, the Conference was adjourned. In the middle of July, Wavell was compelled to announce failure. This time, Congress could not be blamed for the breakdown. Lists of proposed members of the new Executive Council had been obtained from all parties except the Muslim League. As a last resort, Wavell made his own proposed selection of Muslim League names, but the solution was rejected by the Muslim leader, Jinnah.

Today, we may reflect that there was something extraordinary about all these Indian constitutional wrangles. Small numbers of British politicians, and small numbers of Indian politicians, were debating the future of a subcontinent whose people were overwhelmingly illiterate, voteless, desperately poor peasants. Most of the conspicuous Indian leaders, including Gandhi and Nehru, Jinnah and Bose, had been educated in Britain, and their political ideas were profoundly influenced by British thought. Yet to the great majority of the people who would be affected, concepts like 'India' or 'Pakistan' or 'Dominion Status' must have been incomprehensible. The arguments between the various politicians mostly concerned constitutional matters, while the overwhelming needs of the majority of Indians – Hindu and Muslim alike – were economic, as the terrible Bengal famine brought out so clearly.

*

Ceylon (now Sri Lanka) was subjected to air raids, but the Japanese made no attempt to conquer the island. In the later part of the war, there was much discussion about its constitutional future. In 1931, Ceylon had received a new Constitution, which granted a wide measure of responsible government and adult franchise. As the war proceeded, the demand for full Dominion status grew. In 1943, a declaration from the British Government promised substantial advances in that direction, but these were not regarded as sufficient by the country's Ministers, who sent further proposals to the Colonial Office early in 1944.

The Ceylon Ministers were able to make the running in discussion about their country's future for a rather technical reason. The British Government was anxious to avoid elections to the State Council for the duration of the war. In the middle of 1944, the life of the existing State Council had already been extended for four years beyond its normal limit. Any further extension would require assent of the Ministers; otherwise, a General Election would follow automatically in January 1945. The Ministers refused to give that assent unless progress was made with constitutional proposals for the future. So the British Government decided to appoint what later became known as the Soulbury Commission to review the matter.[10]

At this point, further trouble arose between the British Government and the Ceylon Ministers. The Soulbury Commission was required to consult, *inter alia*, the various minority groups in Ceylon. The Ministers, who, with one exception, belonged to the Sinhalese majority, resented that provision. Somehow, an early General Election was averted nevertheless, and the Commission reported shortly after the end of the war – a matter which will call for attention later.

*

At the turn of 1944–45, Allied troops began driving the Japanese out of Burma. Aung San, who had given such substantial help to the enemy three years earlier, was currently in charge of the Burmese army. At that point he made secret contact with the British, and in March 1945 dramatically switched sides. The political organisation with which he was associated was soon incorporated in an Advisory Council which the British military authorities set up.

When Japan surrendered on 14 August 1945, her forces still occupied much of the Allied territory they had seized in 1941–42, while other parts were under Allied military control. It was not immediately clear whether the Japanese would lay down arms everywhere, as they were apparently required to do. Late in August, however, a formal agreement was reached and ratified a few days later, enabling the Allies to reoccupy their former territories in South-East Asia. So far as British possessions were concerned, the process was completed during September, and in most places – Hong Kong was briefly an exception – this took place without serious incident.

The Japanese conflict had caused, or at least had catalysed, developments which would have enormous repercussions in the British Empire in Asia in the next few years. A non-European Power had cut through that Empire, and through other European Empires, like a knife through butter. Japan had indeed been defeated, but only by a more massive combination of enemies than had ever been known in history, assisted in the end by the completely new technology of atomic power. Why should Asians continue to acknowledge European domination in their own affairs? It was certain that there would be substantial and rapid moves everywhere in the direction of self-government, and some of the places would become more or less completely independent. Whether the various countries which were currently part of the British Empire would be called 'Dominions' or not, they would certainly not look towards Britain with the almost family feelings which Australia, Canada and New Zealand had been wont to show.

Yet in the major Allied countries, the British Empire was apparently regarded as a quasi-permanent institution, right to the end of the war. At Yalta in February 1945, and at Potsdam in July and August, the British head of government met his American and Soviet counterparts on a footing of at least nominal equality. This rôle could hardly have been claimed on behalf of a nation with population of only 50 some million, and resources that bore no comparison with those of either the United States or the Soviet Union. It was evidently based on the assumption that Britain was still in a real sense the leader of a great Empire.

5
Aftermath

Many important decisions about the Empire and its future had been made by the All-Party Coalition Government. Some of those decisions carried implications for the future; but new problems were certain to arise, which would need to be handled by a different administration. When Germany surrendered in May 1945, the Coalition Government broke up and machinery was set in motion for a General Election. A 'Caretaker Government', consisting mainly of Conservatives, was established to deal with urgent matters. Votes were counted late in July and resulted in a large Labour majority. Churchill resigned, and Clement Attlee, leader of the Labour Party, became Prime Minister.

Decisions about the future of India would be critical not only for the subcontinent but for many other places as well, and matters were now beginning to acquire increasing urgency. The new Government, like its recent predecessors, believed that India should become a self-governing Dominion. Whether that line of development was possible or not, some action on the Indian constitution would be required in the near future. In September 1945, the Viceroy told the Labour Cabinet that Nehru and other major Congress leaders 'contemplate recourse sooner or later to force in order to secure their goal of complete independence'.[1] The new Government had no intention of being driven into a false position by an Indian initiative of that kind. Later in the month, it was announced that elections for the central and provincial legislatures would be held in the forthcoming cold season. Thereafter a constitution-making body, the Constituent Assembly, would be convened.

Party attitudes were immediately struck in India. Congress insisted that India must become an independent state. The Muslim League demanded 'Pakistan'. Among minority religions, the Sikhs made it plain that they abhorred the idea of a separate Pakistan. They had every reason to fear being caught in a savage power-struggle between two larger factions. Spokesmen for the Depressed Castes pointed out that the legislatures would be profoundly unrepresentative, since more than 90 per cent of Indians were denied the vote.

Indian views continued to harden. Early in November, trials of members of Bose's Indian National Army commenced in Delhi. Soon one Provincial Governor was urging Wavell to

> wipe the whole thing out and take no further proceedings against anyone ... I think that every day that passes now brings over more and more well disposed Indians into the anti-British camp.[2]

Wavell took the point, and cabled the new Secretary of State to that effect the same day.[3] There are some parallels with the aftermath of the 1916 rising in Dublin. In many minds the INA was beginning to acquire the status of a patriotic movement.

Results of the Central Legislative Assembly elections were announced on the first day of 1946. Of 102 elected members, Congress returned 56, the Muslim League 30. Provincial elections were held a little later, and Congress secured an overall majority in eight of the eleven Provinces. Finally, voting for the Constituent Assembly took place in July. Of 296 seats from 'British India', Congress won 202, the Muslim League 73. The Princely States would nominate the remaining 93. In 'British India', politics had become a simple confrontation between Congress and the Muslim League, with nobody else counting for much.

While these various elections were proceeding, the British Government announced that a special Mission of Cabinet Ministers would be sent to India. It would work with the Viceroy and would have discussions with leaders of Indian opinion about problems arising out of self-government. As the Constituent Assembly was deeply split on the matter of India's future, the Mission and the Viceroy soon felt obliged to submit proposals of their own. The idea of a separate Pakistan was rejected. Figures were produced which left no doubt that, however Pakistan might be defined, great numbers of non-Muslims would be included, while many millions of Muslims would be left out. The Mission suggested that Muslim apprehensions might be allayed in a different way. The central government, which would cover both 'British India' and the Princely States, would deal only with foreign affairs, defence and communications and raising the finance necessary for those purposes, while other matters would be vested in the individual Provinces or States. These suggestions were not accepted by the Indian politicians, but the British Cabinet judged that they 'now for the first time seemed to accept the sincerity of our efforts on India's behalf'.[4]

The prospect of persuading the Constituent Assembly to agree a constitution continued to recede, and Wavell became increasingly alarmed about the probable consequences of failure. At the end of 1946, he warned that 'we are not in a position to maintain British rule in India beyond 31 March 1948, and possibly not for so long', and went on to declare that 'we may at any time be involved in what is virtually a civil war between Hindus and Muslims'.[5] The alternatives, he argued, were 'to withdraw from India or to reassert our authority'. Withdrawal he visualised as an operation 'planned on the lines of a military evacuation from hostile territory'.[6] 'Reasserting authority' implied a declaration of intention to govern India for at least a further period of fifteen years, and would need reinforcements of four or five divisions.[7] This, as Wavell presumably realised, was just a theoretical possibility, and politically out of the question. The necessary troops were probably not available. Even if they could somehow be found, the British public would have been unwilling to countenance the cost in life and money that would be entailed. Yet 'withdrawal' in the manner suggested would not only be a calamity for India, but would have appalling consequences for British prestige elsewhere in the world. The Cabinet was nevertheless assured that plans existed for evacuating British troops and civilians from India 'in an extreme emergency'.[8]

As a last hope of averting something like a military withdrawal, the Cabinet decided, against Wavell's advice, to issue a public declaration of intent to transfer power to responsible Indian hands by a date not later than June 1948.[9]

For a considerable time, the Prime Minister had been giving active consideration to replacing Wavell, and had put out feelers before the end of 1946.[10] The successor chosen was Lord Mountbatten. A kinsman of the King, with a most impressive wartime record as Supreme Allied Commander, S.E. Asia, Mountbatten had a more sanguine temperament than his predecessor. The new Viceroy's biographer summarises his terms of appointment succinctly: 'Keep India united if you can; if not, try to save something from the wreck; whatever happens get Britain out.'[11]

Mountbatten's first impressions were bleak indeed:

> The scene here is one of unrelieved gloom. At this early stage I can see little common ground on which to build any agreed solution for the future of India.[12]

As time went on, the picture improved very considerably; but Mountbatten's efforts to save India from partition failed. 'All the Indian Parties,' the Prime Minister told the Cabinet in May,

> were now convinced that, in view of the recalcitrant attitude of the Muslim League, some form of partition was unavoidable. But the Congress view was that, if partition was to be conceded, it was a necessary corollary that there should also be a division of Bengal and the Punjab.[13]

Even after this, Mountbatten made one further unavailing attempt to secure agreement on the basis of retaining a united India.

There were further problems. Mahomed Jinnah, the Muslim League leader, had long contended that Pakistan would wish to become a Dominion; but the view of Congress was that India should become a Republic. The distinction between the two concepts was a good deal sharper in 1947 than it later became; and if one successor-state went one way and the other went in a different way, the division of India would present considerable difficulties, notably with the Civil Service and the Army. A compromise was soon reached, however. As the British were prepared to withdraw from India substantially earlier than the 1948 date originally proposed, Congress was persuaded to allow India to assume, for the time being at least, the status of a Dominion.

Two great Provinces, Bengal and the Punjab, contained both Hindus and Muslims in large numbers. Both were divided, and a

Boundary Commission adjudicated on the line. A Muslim sliver of the predominantly Hindu Province of Assam was also allocated to Pakistan. The new country was to include modern Bangladesh. The Islamic state would thus consist of two areas with widely different languages and cultures, separated by several hundred miles of the new India.

The Princely States were given the chance of adherence to either India or Pakistan. There was a third option of independence, but the British leaned strongly against that one. Deep problems soon surfaced in Hyderabad, which had a Hindu majority but a Muslim ruler, and in Kashmir & Jammu, where matters were the other way round. In Kashmir, the matter has not been fully resolved to this day. Travancore, a State which had a record of progressive government and a high level of literacy, seriously considered declaring independence,[14] but eventually joined India.

Indian independence also posed a political problem at home. The changed status would require an Act of Parliament, and the end of the Parliamentary session was in sight. If the necessary measure proved contentious, there was no way of passing the legislation in time. The matter was resolved by an agreement between the parties, which allowed Indian independence to proceed to enactment without a division in either House. Probably Churchill, who remained the Conservative leader, considered that his party's commitment to the 'Cripps offer' of 1942 precluded any other course of action.

And so, on 15 August 1947, ten weeks after the Viceroy's last effort to avert the split, the great change took place. The Empire of India was extinguished, the Royal title 'Emperor of India' abolished. The country was divided into the successor-states. In an extraordinary compliment to the last Viceroy, India chose Mountbatten as Governor-General. On this basis, the enormous problems associated with Indian independence were eventually resolved at almost breakneck speed and with general assent, though scarcely enthusiasm, from the various politicians involved.

How did the matter look to ordinary Indians? A few months earlier, Attlee reflected that

It has been common ground with all of us who have had to study the Indian problem that there are millions of Indians who do not really wish for a change of government but they are passive. The active elements in the population, including practically all the educated classes, have been indoctrinated to a greater or lesser degree with nationalism.[15]

Very soon, however, the 'silent majority' was profoundly affected by the transition. There had been many outbreaks of communal violence before the split took place, and in the immediate aftermath there were massacres and counter-massacres on a huge scale. Gandhi himself was assassinated by a Hindu fanatic in 1948.

*

Indian independence was bound to influence events elsewhere. As long ago as 1931, when the proposal that Burma should be split from India was being mooted, the then Secretary of State for India had promised that Burma would not lag behind India in constitutional development. The Constitution which Burma received later in the decade was not particularly successful. In the judgement of the Governor, the Ministers and House of Representatives were of poor quality, while 'politics both local and national [were] hopelessly corrupt'.[16] Then the country came under Japanese military occupation, which many Burmese supported, and was the scene of two major military campaigns, while the immediate post-war period was marked by great economic difficulties.

In the concluding phase of the Far Eastern war, Aung San was immensely popular, and – in the Governor's view – 'the most important figure in Burma'.[17] In the immediate aftermath, there was a great deal of jockeying between different Burmese politicians, in which Aung San and his 'Anti-Fascist People's Freedom League' (AFPFL) played a leading part. After much argument, representatives from most of the leading Burmese political movements joined the Governor's Executive Council. Towards the end of 1946, the Executive Council was invited to send representatives to London for discussions about the country's future. The delegation, headed by Aung San, arrived in January 1947, and it was soon agreed that the Executive Council should function as an Interim Government, which would be treated like the government of a Dominion. A Constituent Assembly was to be elected in the ensuing spring to devise the country's eventual constitution.

The Constituent Assembly elections were boycotted by several leading politicians, including Ba Maw and U Saw, but they produced a large overall majority for the AFPFL. In June, the Assembly adopted unanimously a resolution moved by Aung San, calling for the country to become 'an independent sovereign Republic'. Later in the month, a Goodwill Mission, headed by Aung San's second-in-command, U Nu, formerly known as Thakin Nu, arrived in London. Like his chief, Nu had been a major figure in the Burmese régime which cooperated with Japan during the occupation. According to the Prime Minister's statement to the British Cabinet,

> The members of the Mission would themselves have been in favour of Burma's remaining in the British Commonwealth, but ... saw no prospect that either their own supporters or Burmese opinion generally could be brought to accept anything less than independence outside the Commonwealth.[18]

Whatever the Cabinet may have thought about the sincerity of these protestations, it decided to set in motion the necessary British legislation. It is a matter of speculation whether Burma might have acted differently if the possibility of becoming a Republic within the Commonwealth had been conceived at the time.

On 19 July 1947, when plans were being made to implement the recent agreement, armed men assassinated seven members of the Executive Council, including Aung San. By coincidence, U Nu was not present at the time and he was invited to form a new government. Both U Saw and Ba Maw were arrested in connection with the murders. Ba Maw was later released, but U Saw was sentenced to death and eventually executed. In the shadow of these inauspicious events, Burmese independence was proclaimed on 4 January 1948.

British political attitudes were very different from those that marked the Indian independence legislation a few months earlier. Churchill declared the Government's action to be a 'policy of scuttle'. Survivors of the 'forgotten army' which Britain had sent to liberate Burma from the Japanese must have been astonished to see the country handed over to an administration headed by an erstwhile collaborator with that enemy. The recent assassinations suggested that any government there was likely to be highly unstable, and a military takeover might occur at any moment. No thinking person in Burma or in Britain could have contemplated the country's future without profound misgivings. Yet, in retrospect, it is difficult to see how any British Government could have acted very differently.

*

The post-war fate of Ceylon was necessarily influenced by happenings in India and Burma, but the course of events there was markedly different from both. The Soulbury Commission which had been appointed during the war reported in October 1945. A new constitution was devised, following broadly the Soulbury recommendations, and was announced in May 1946. A bicameral parliament would be set up, with powers in many ways corresponding with those of a Dominion, but without authority to discriminate against minority religious groups and with only limited powers in matters of defence and external relations. In September, in the first elections under the new constitution, Communists and their allies secured something like 40 per cent of the seats in the lower house: an alarming state of affairs, in view of the 'Cold War' conditions which were already developing.

The qualifications to full independence raised considerable difficulties in both Ceylon and Britain. In the view of the Colonial Secretary, the country's Prime Minister D.S. Senanayake, was 'seriously embarrassed' by domestic criticism of what was deemed the 'inferior' constitutional status accorded to his country, by comparison with India and Burma.[19] On the other side, the British Chiefs of Staff, worried about the country's strategic importance, pressed for adequate safeguards.[20]

In the course of 1947, a compromise gradually evolved. Ceylon received legislative powers in all matters; while an acceptable defence agreement was reached with the country's government. The appropriate legislation passed through the British parliament without difficulty, and Ceylon received full independence as a Dominion in February 1948.

In 1944, the Cabinet had considered the future of other Asian territories which Japan had overrun earlier in the war and which had not yet been restored to British control. Particular attention was given to Malaya and Borneo.[21] In both cases, the state of affairs before the Japanese attack had been complex, and throws light on the idiosyncratic arrangements which prevailed in various parts of the British Empire before the war.

Malaya had been divided into the Straits Settlements, which included Singapore and was administered as a colony, and the nine Malay States. These fell into two groups, the 'Federated' and 'Unfederated' States. All were administered by local rulers, or Sultans, who were subject to varying measures of influence and control by Britain. Thus, in a country with about five million inhabitants, there were ten more or less independent political entities, with little or no sense of common nationality. This state of affairs was a consequence of the haphazard growth of Empire in the nineteenth and early twentieth centuries. It made less and less sense as time went on. The war had brought out the glaring inadequacy of military defence. The muddles, or worse, which were revealed during the Japanese attack were famous enough. It was equally clear that the multiplicity of more or less sovereign political units, most of them ruled under anachronistic political systems, hampered the economy and the prosperity of the people. On top of this there was a huge ethnic problem. Indigenous Malays and immigrant Chinese were present in approximately equal numbers, and there were also many people of Indian stock living in the country.

During the war, Malaya was occupied by Japan, except for the four 'Unfederated' States which reverted to Thailand. The British Government made plans for the future, designed to create a greater measure of unity and to transfer much authority from the various unrepresentative individuals and bodies who controlled parts of the area, to the Colonial Office. This, however, was not a matter on which British authorities could freely decide, for various treaties and other arrangements had been made with the Malay rulers, which could not be lightly disregarded. So complex negotiations were set in train.

When the Japanese war ended, Malaya was put under military control. Meanwhile, more detailed plans were made for the future. The original idea of the new Labour Government, set out in a White Paper of January 1946, was to create a constitutional union, with common citizenship. According to this plan, Malaya would initially become something like a colony, while eventually British rule would be replaced by self-government. The Sultans would keep their titles, incomes and religious functions, but would lose most of their political authority. A Special Envoy, Sir Harold MacMichael, was despatched from London to secure support, or at least acquiescence, of the Sultans.

Initially, these approaches appeared to have been successful and the rulers gave their assent. Then, in March 1946, a body known as the United Malays National Organisation (UMNO) came into existence, expressing a sharp popular Malay reaction against 'common citizenship' proposals. The Sultans back-pedalled on their initial acceptance. By the end of 1946, the British Cabinet had decided that the original 'Malayan Union' plans would need to be abandoned in favour of a much looser 'Federation of Malaya'.[22] Singapore, whose immense strategic and economic importance still remained, but which had an overwhelmingly Chinese population, would need to be treated separately from the peninsula, at least for the time being,[23] and become a separate Crown Colony.

The new arrangements for Malaya were put into effect in February 1948. The Federal Government was headed by a British High Commissioner, appointed with approval of the Sultans. Nominated Executive and Legislative Councils were set up. State governments with considerable powers were established, headed by Sultans in the old Malay States and by Resident Commissioners in the two remaining Straits Settlements, Penang and Malacca.

This time it was the Chinese who reacted sharply, and violence broke out. At first it was not clear how far the trouble was the work of robber gangs and how far it was politically directed; but it soon turned into an armed revolt dominated by a body known as the Malayan People's Anti-Japanese Army. The MPAJA had come into existence during the war, as a Communist-led partisan body. In practice it was composed almost exclusively of people of Chinese stock and was shunned by the Malays, who had long felt threatened by Chinese immigration. When the war ended, the MPAJA did not disband. By 1948, 'Cold War' conditions had completely replaced the wartime alliance between the Soviet Union and the Western Democracies, and so the new conflict acquired international as well as imperial overtones.

In June 1948, a 'State of Emergency' was declared in Malaya and in Singapore. The rebel forces were never very numerous, but attacked and frequently killed people, particularly those connected with the rubber estates and tin mines. The most dangerous moment was in October 1951, when the British High Commissioner was murdered. Oliver Lyttleton, who became Colonial Secretary soon afterwards, decided that the successor should combine political and military headship.[24] General Sir Gerald Templer was appointed to both posts early in 1952, and by the time his command ended a couple of years later the revolt was under control, though the Emergency did not end officially until 1960.

The long-term future of Malaya was linked closely with that of Borneo. Before the war, the south of the island was part of the Dutch East Indies; but in the north there were four distinct territories which ranked as parts of the British Empire. British North Borneo (Sabah) was controlled by a Chartered Company, redolent of the old East India Company and the more recent British South Africa Company. Brunei had an indigenous ruler, but there were provisions for a resident British adviser, whose recommendations had to be followed on important matters of policy. Sarawak, more independent than Brunei, had been administered by a succession of 'white rajahs' of the Brooke family since 1842. The little island of Labuan, offshore from Brunei, had passed from one kind of British administration to another on several occasions in the previous century, but was currently part of the Straits Settlements. Thus the political links of Labuan were not with any part of Borneo, but Malaya.

In 1944, the Coalition Cabinet had considered the future of British territories in Borneo, thinking – as with Malaya – that the various local anomalies might be ironed out. Labuan might easily be detached from the Straits Settlements and incorporated in one of the other Borneo territories; but elsewhere (as in Malaya) there were greater difficulties because of treaty rights vested in the ruling authorities.

North Borneo and Sarawak had suffered much damage during the war and had no prospect of repairing that damage from their own resources. The authorities of North Borneo were easily persuaded to accept the new status of a Crown Colony. Sarawak was more difficult. The ruling Rajah, Sir Charles Vyner Brooke, appreciated that it was impossible for his regime to rehabilitate the Territory, and was willing that it should also be annexed to the Crown. He also did not wish his heir presumptive to succeed as Rajah, so had the added incentive of a family quarrel. Yet not only did the heir object to the change, but so also did many local people. In the end, however, the Council Negri accepted the proposed change by a narrow majority, and in July 1946 Sarawak became a Crown Colony.[25]

*

An important change took place much closer to Britain in the late 1940s. The ambiguous status of Éire from 1937 onwards has already been noted. The Irish General Election of 1948 brought to an end the long rule of de Valera's Fianna Fáil Party, and gave control to a coalition under John Costello, with Fine Gael as the leading element. Traditionally, Fine Gael had been more pro-British than its rival, and in September 1948 there was considerable astonishment when Costello announced that he was seeking to declare Éire a Republic. The only formal link remaining with Britain was Éire's External Relations Act of 1936, which recognised the King's authority to appoint Irish diplomatic representatives abroad on the advice of the Éire Government. The Dáil was persuaded, without difficulty, to repeal the measure. In April 1949, the formal break took place.

*

The experience of both Éire and Burma had shown that it was possible for a country to secede from the Commonwealth and become a Republic. When India prepared to devise a Constitution in the late 1940s, it soon became evident that this document would proclaim the country a 'sovereign independent republic'. It therefore seemed likely that India would also leave the Commonwealth. Current constitutional theory supported that view. The Statute of Westminster had declared members of the Commonwealth to be 'united by a common allegiance to the Crown', which would clearly not apply to India.

Yet there were also indications that the governments of both India and Britain wished to preserve some sort of link. Prime Minister Attlee set up a small group of ministers to consider whether this was possible. Contact was made with the governments of Australia, Canada and New Zealand, who also wished a link with India to be preserved. The Prime Minister reported to the Cabinet in October 1948 and it was immediately obvious that considerable difficulties existed. Further study revealed more problems still.[26] There were likely to be considerable difficulties with domestic opinion in Britain and some

Commonwealth countries if India became a Republic. There might also be difficulties with foreign countries. Many commercial treaties contained a 'most-favoured-nation' clause, which authorised the other partner to require treatment not less favourable than that which Britain afforded to any other foreign state. Internal Commonwealth arrangements, like the Ottawa treaties of 1932, were exempt from operation of this clause, because Commonwealth countries shared an allegiance to the Crown. If Britain and the Indian Republic made new preferential trading arrangements, or even sought to continue existing arrangements, would this activate 'most-favoured-nation' clauses? Legal opinion appeared unclear as to how far the difficulty would be met. But the experience of Burma, and growing fears about risks from international communism, strongly encouraged ministers to seek a solution which would retain some kind of link with India.

High-level discussions about possible ways of meeting such problems ran on for months. Attlee made contact with British Opposition leaders, who evidently shared his own wishes on the matter. As for the task of convincing the wider Commonwealth, a meeting of Commonwealth Prime Ministers was held in April 1949, at which all the self-governing countries were represented. Everybody seemed to wish the Commonwealth link to be retained, but it proved exceedingly difficult to devise a wholly satisfactory formula.[27] The Conference eventually acknowledged the Indian Government's 'desire to continue her full membership of the Commonwealth of Nations and her acceptance of the King as the symbol of the free association of its independent member nations and as such the Head of the Commonwealth'. On these terms, the Conference resolved to accept and recognise India's continuing membership.

Even so, two of the Dominions insisted on inserting riders of their own. South Africa, which was moving further away from other Commonwealth countries for a variety of reasons, was anxious to make it clear that the description of the King as 'Head of the Commonwealth' did not imply that he discharged any constitutional function by virtue of that position. Pakistan required assurance that if she, in due course, also became a republic, it would also be open to her to remain in the Commonwealth. A few weeks later, the Indian Constituent Assembly approved the arrangements which had been hammered out with so much difficulty. On 26 January 1950, the new Republic was inaugurated.

India's new status also affected the Courts of Law. Like other Commonwealth countries of the period, India had still permitted appeals from its own Courts to the Judicial Committee of the Privy Council in London. Thus, Gandhi's assassin appealed unsuccessfully to the Privy Council against his conviction by an Indian Court as late as 1949. Nobody seemed to dispute the fairness of the Privy Council, or even the convenience of the arrangement from India's point of view; but considerations of national pride took precedence and the right of appeal from Indian courts was finally removed. Many other Commonwealth countries would later do the same, though some retain the right of appeal to this day.

India continued to cooperate with Britain in many fields; but one important change was associated with the country's new status. The Dominions had usually followed the British lead in matters of defence and foreign policy, and when Éire decided to remain neutral in 1939 she ceased to be treated as a Dominion. The new Republic of India rapidly struck out in an independent direction. In the early 1950s, the 'Cold War' was at its height, and the world was divided ever more deeply between countries which looked to the United States and Britain and those which looked to the Soviet Union. India took a neutralist stance, which became obvious when the Korean War began later in 1950.

During the brief period when India ranked as a Dominion, a curious issue arose which seems at first merely verbal, but which may have had some real importance. It derives from Attlee's suggestions at the Commonwealth Prime Ministers' meetings in October 1948.[28] The terms 'Dominion' and 'Dominion status' had been widely used for many years to refer to a country of which the King was Head of State, but which was fully independent and authorised to conduct its own relations with foreign countries. At the end of 1948, Attlee circulated a memorandum to the Cabinet, indicating that both terms should be avoided, and the more uncertain expressions 'Commonwealth country', 'Commonwealth government' or 'member of the Commonwealth' should be used instead in official documents.[29] This recommendation has been followed since, in spite of changes of government, although it seems to have no legal authority. The practical effect has been to blur the distinction between a Dominion and a Republic within the Commonwealth.

6
Ottoman Succession

Some very important new developments of British imperial influence which took place in the aftermath of the 1914–18 war were to have repercussions for many years to come. They had deep roots. The Ottoman, or Turkish, Empire had been gradually disintegrating for many years, and during the nineteenth and early twentieth centuries all the Great Powers were deeply interested in the 'Ottoman succession' – partly because they sought advantages for themselves, perhaps more often because they feared the consequences of others extending their influence. In 1878, Britain acquired effective control[1] over the Turkish island of Cyprus, and from 1882 onwards she became increasingly involved in Egypt, which was still, theoretically, an Ottoman province.

When Turkey entered the war on Germany's side in November 1914, Britain promptly declared formal annexation of Cyprus and proclaimed Egypt a Protectorate. As the Great War proceeded, other Ottoman territories came under close British attention. The Gallipoli expedition of 1915 sought to strike at the very heart of the Ottoman Empire; but it proved a disastrous failure. The Turks unsuccessfully disputed the British position in Egypt. In 1915, when the Allies were busily bribing everybody in sight to enter the war on their side, Cyprus was offered to Greece as an inducement. The King of Greece was pro-German, the bribe was rejected and the offer lapsed. In the later stages of the war, the British launched substantial, and largely successful, military expeditions into the predominantly Arab lands to the south of modern Turkey, which had still been Ottoman at the beginning of the war.

Diplomatic activity in the Arab lands was to have a very long-term effect. The British sought to subvert ambitious Arab leaders to the Allied cause. Sir Henry McMahon, British High Commissioner in Egypt, made contact with Hussein, Sharif of Mecca, to whom he addressed a very significant letter in October 1915. This contained an offer of eventual independence for Arabs in a large part of the area which they occupied, in return for support against the Turks. Whether, on a fair interpretation of the words of the letter, that area included Palestine, was, and remains, a matter of dispute; but there can be little doubt that the Arabs believed, and were intended to believe, that it did so. The offer was highly secret at the time, but the gist gradually leaked out and many years later it was officially published.

Parallel with these discussions, other negotiations took place, involving the three major Allies, Britain, France and Russia. These culminated in the Sykes–Picot Agreement of May 1916, which also was initially highly secret. It proposed a complex division of possessions and influence between the three Powers. The Agreement was published in Russia shortly after the Bolsheviks took charge in November 1917 and was widely considered by Arabs to constitute duplicity on the Allies' part. By the date of the disclosure, however, the Arabs were too deeply committed to the Allied side to do much about it.

A third, and rather later, line of Allied wartime intrigue touched on the Jews. Ever since the 1890s, significant numbers of Jews had been attracted to the idea of 'Zionism' – that they should eventually establish a Jewish state in Palestine. Zionism had particularly strong roots among Jews in Russia, where the Tsarist Government had an appalling record of persecution.

Early in 1917 the Russian Tsar was deposed. The Allies hoped that the new Republic would fight the war with more competence and vigour, but this did not happen. By the early autumn of that year, Russia was in a state of near-collapse. Soldiers were 'voting with their feet', and deserting wholesale. Furthermore, as the Foreign Secretary Arthur Balfour explained to the Cabinet, 'the German government were making great efforts to capture the sympathy of the Zionist movement'.[2] A little later he reported the view that 'the vast majority of Jews in Russia and America, as, indeed, all over the world, now appeared to be favourable to Zionism'.[3] Balfour was in close contact with the academic chemist Dr Chaim Weizmann, an enthusiastic Zionist on whose judgement the Foreign Secretary may well have relied to a considerable extent.

British Jews, by contrast, were by no means all Zionists. Edwin Montagu, Secretary for India, was the only Jew holding major government office. He told the Cabinet that the one trial of strength between Zionists and anti-Zionists in England had resulted in only a very narrow majority for the Zionists.[4] The difference between Russian Jews and many British Jews is not difficult to understand. Montagu was proud to declare himself a 'Jewish Englishman'; few of his co-religionists in Russia can have felt similar enthusiasm for being members of a state that treated them so badly.

Whatever the true strength of Zionism might be, the British Government was eager to outflank German propaganda. Lord Milner, a member of Lloyd George's War Cabinet, proposed a Declaration in terms very similar to those which would eventually be used by Balfour, recommending 'the establishment in Palestine of a National Home for the Jewish race'. An important qualification was that 'nothing shall be done which may prejudice the civil and religious rights of existing non-Jewish communities in Palestine'.[5] Milner's draft was submitted confidentially to President Wilson of the United States, and to Jews of both Zionist and anti-Zionist persuasion.

At the end of October, the proposed Declaration was again debated in the War Cabinet.[6] This time, Balfour was authorised to issue it, with a few minor changes of wording from Milner's original draft. As with the McMahon letter, the exact meaning of some crucial words in the Balfour Declaration was unclear. Nor is it certain whether the two offers were really reconcilable.

The deepest irony of the Balfour Declaration was its timing. It was issued on 2 November 1917, in the form of a letter from the Foreign Secretary to Lord Rothschild, the distinguished Jewish banker – famous also as a naturalist. Just five days later, the Bolsheviks in St Petersburg overthrew Kerensky's 'Provisional Government' and shortly afterwards sued for peace with Germany. So the object of rallying Russian Jews to the Allied cause, which appears to have been the main purpose of the whole operation, had already ceased to have any importance within a week of publication of the Balfour Declaration.

At the end of the Great War and for several years after, the future of many places which had been, at least in name, part of the

Ottoman Empire before 1914 was debated. In Egypt, there were serious anti-British riots early in 1919. Eventually, General Allenby, who had played a major part in driving the Turks from the Arab lands during the war, was sent to Cairo. His policy was conciliatory – perhaps unexpectedly so – and by the closing months of the year matters had quietened down considerably. A British mission of inquiry was then sent out and recommended that the protectorate should be replaced by a bilateral treaty. A long period of argument followed, but eventually the recommendation was accepted and, in February 1922, Egypt was formally declared 'an independent sovereign state'. This was a very qualified independence, however; for the same instrument reserved for Britain such matters as Imperial communications in Egypt, military defence of the country and control over the Sudan.

Cyprus was affected in a different way. Greek-speaking people formed a large majority of the island's population, and the great issue was whether it should have *enosis*, or union, with Greece. There was a good historical precedent for Britain voluntarily ceding Greek-speaking territory to the Greek state, for the Ionian Islands had been relinquished in 1864. But antagonism between Greeks and Turks had been endemic for hundreds of years, and the idea of *enosis* appalled the Turkish minority and also some important elements of British opinion. In 1919, the War Cabinet discussed the matter, but reached no definite conclusion.[7]

The future of the Arab lands which had belonged to the Ottoman Empire was disputed between many parties. Various Arab leaders, including Hussein, Sharif of Mecca, his sons, and Ibn Saud, eponymous founder of Saudi Arabia, all sought to carve out kingdoms for themselves. Disputes arose between Arabs and Europeans, among the Arabs and among the Europeans. The British and French were often at loggerheads.

The new League of Nations distributed Mandates over former enemy territory to various Allied countries. The Mandatory Powers undertook the responsibility, acting on the League's behalf, to promote the 'wellbeing and development' of the indigenous peoples, as a 'sacred trust for civilization'. Britain received Mandates over the former Ottoman territories of Palestine and Mesopotamia (later known as Iraq). Palestine, as originally understood, was soon divided into the territory west of the Jordan which then became generally known as Palestine, and the territory to the east which became known as Transjordan. At this time the population of Palestine was around 750,000, of whom about 78 per cent were Arabs:[8] mainly settled peasants or town-dwellers, but a substantial number of them nomadic Bedouin. Jews numbered 84,000, or about 11 per cent of the whole.

As far back as April 1920, the Allied Supreme Council had prescribed that Britain should be responsible for giving effect to the Balfour Declaration.[9] An announcement was soon made that up to 16,500 Jews were to be admitted in the following year. There was immediate Arab alarm, and considerable disturbances soon followed. In one sense this was surprising, for traditionally Muslims and Jews had got on quite well. What concerned the Arabs in this case, however, was the fear that great numbers of people very different from themselves would soon enter Palestine and change the whole character of the country. Various British attempts were made to allay Arab fears, and for much of the 1920s the ethnic problems of Palestine seemed, on the whole, to die down. In 1927, there was actually more Jewish emigration than immigration.

Transjordan was not affected by the Balfour Declaration, and the British Mandate worked successfully in the early post-war period. Abdullah, son of Hussein of Mecca, was appointed Emir. In 1927 the country received a qualified independence, although the British Mandate remained for a long time to come and British influence for longer still.

Iraq had a turbulent early history. Feisal, brother of Abdullah of Transjordan, had first sought to establish a kingdom for himself in Syria, but he was expelled by the French, who were the Mandatory Power. He was then encouraged by the British, becoming accepted as Emir, and later King, of Iraq. Much trouble followed, but in 1922 a Treaty was concluded with Britain, which gave the Mandatory Power large authority over military, judicial and financial affairs. A new Treaty was later negotiated, which took effect in 1932. The Mandate was terminated, and Iraq was acknowledged as an independent state and a member of the League of Nations. Britain was authorised to station troops in Iraq, but it was made clear that this did not constitute 'occupation'. As in Transjordan, strong British influence remained for many years. In some former Ottoman lands, Britain acquired influence of a less formal kind. Saudi Arabia, whose immensely valuable oil reserves were still unknown, came to rely on a British subsidy, while the small Arab states and sheikhdoms of the Persian Gulf also looked to British support.[10]

Ethnic violence in Palestine, which seemed to be subsiding during much of the 1920s, suddenly flared up again in 1929. Then there was some abatement. But persecution of Jews in Europe, and particularly in Germany from 1933 onwards, gave a great boost to Jewish immigration to Palestine. In 1934, for example, the number of Jewish immigrants – legal and illegal – is said to have exceeded 60,000.[11] Predictably, this exacerbated tension between Jews and Arabs.

In April 1936, Arab terrorists attacked Jews in Jaffa, and almost immediately there was Jewish retaliation. Soon there were widespread disorders, which induced the British Government to set up a Royal Commission to make recommendations. The Commission's eventual Report, published in July 1937, proposed, among other things, that Palestine should be partitioned into a Jewish state, an Arab state and a neutral enclave, which would include Jerusalem and Bethlehem. The partition proposal was highly contentious, and there was considerable opposition in both Arab and Jewish communities.

By 1939, the total population of Palestine had approximately doubled since Britain assumed responsibility, standing at around 1.5 million. The absolute numbers of all ethnic groups had increased, but there were now 445,000 Jews, or nearly 30 per cent of the whole population. Economically, this immigration probably benefited the Arabs considerably (as the substantial rise in Arab numbers suggests); but this did not detract from their growing feeling of apprehension about the future. There was also considerable ill-feeling among Arabs themselves, particularly against Arab landlords who had sold estates to immigrant Jews.

Efforts were made to persuade Arabs and Jews to reach a mutually acceptable solution about Palestine's future, but they failed to do so, and the British Government decided to impose a solution of its own. In May 1939, an important statement of British policy in Palestine was issued in the form of a White Paper.[12] Several policy objectives were indicated, including the creation of an independent Palestinian state in which Arabs and Jews would share, within ten years. What would prove most important, however, was the recommendation that Jewish immigration should be permitted at the rate of 15,000 a year over the next five years; whereafter no further immigration would be permitted unless the Arabs agreed. In the view of the Colonial Secretary, this would eventually provide a basis for the two communities to live side by side. Like all other proposals, the White Paper recommendations were contentious, and the Permanent Mandates Commission of the League of Nations decided, by four votes to three, that the policy was incompatible with the requirements of the Mandate. Britain nevertheless went ahead with its declared policy.

While turbulent world events of the middle and late 1930s exacerbated relations between Britons, Arabs and Jews in Palestine, they gave some relief to the tensions in Egypt. Ending the formal British Protectorate in 1922 had not been followed by smooth relations and there were repeated Egyptian demands for real independence. But dangers revealed by the Italo-Abyssinian conflict of 1935–36 made Britain more willing to make concessions to Egypt, while Egyptians perceived a long-term threat to their own country, which could be resisted most effectively by British military support.

From this emerged the Anglo-Egyptian Treaty of 1936, which gave Egypt a substantially greater measure of real independence and was more or less universally accepted by Egyptian politicians. The Treaty was to last for 20 years. It reserved to Britain the right to keep 10,000 troops in the Canal Zone in peacetime, and many more in war. Provision was also made for restoration of Egyptian influence in the Sudan. In the following year, Egypt was admitted to the League of Nations and was authorised to set up its own embassies and consulates.

When war came in 1939, problems of the Middle East were seen essentially from a military rather than a diplomatic angle. In the following year, Italy invaded Egypt from bases in her colony Libya, and the British Government resolved to resist the attack. Something like 500,000 Allied troops eventually entered the country and much of Egypt became a battlefield. As time went on, relations between the British and Egyptian Governments became worse, though the presence of so many Allied troops made an effective action against the occupying authority impossible.

In Palestine, by contrast, ethnic tensions which had plagued the British authorities for so long were somewhat reduced. Not many European Jews were able to escape to Palestine from Nazi persecution, and the White Paper quota of 75,000 immigrants over a five-year period had not been reached when the war came to an end. In the last stages of the European war, the horrors of the Holocaust were suddenly understood by the public in Allied and enemy countries alike.

Shortly after the war ended, Ernest Bevin, Foreign Secretary in the new Labour Government, enunciated principles which should govern future British policy in the Middle East. It was, so he told the Cabinet,

> essential to broaden the basis of British influence in the Middle East by developing an economic and social policy which would make for prosperity and contentment in the area as a whole. It would be the object of this policy to remedy the mal-distribution of purchasing power in the Middle Eastern countries and to raise the standard of living of the masses of the people.[13]

If that policy had been set into effect 20 years earlier, it might have had most salutary consequences; but it was already much too late for Britain to implement it. Throughout the Middle East, events were already taking charge.

Almost immediately attention turned to Egypt. The Anglo-Egyptian Treaty of 1936 provided for possible revision after ten years, and at the end of 1945 the Egyptian Government applied for such revision. Egypt sought the withdrawal of all British forces from her territory, and reduction – perhaps extinction – of British influence in the Sudan. The official diplomatic approach was soon reinforced by popular rioting in Egypt.

The question of the Sudan had been troubling statesmen for many years and would continue to do so for some time to come. British involvement dated from the 1880s, when the celebrated General Gordon waged his disastrous campaign against 'the Mahdi'. In the aftermath, British, Egyptian and French interests were all involved, until the Anglo-Egyptian Convention of 1899, sometimes known as the Condominium Agreement, recognised joint British and Egyptian sovereignty over the Sudan.[14] The respective rights of the two co-domini, and of the Sudanese themselves, were frequently at issue thereafter. Matters were more or less regularised by the Anglo-Egyptian agreement of 1936. As for the immediate question of Anglo-Egyptian relations, which would be likely to affect the whole Nile valley, Egypt and the Sudan alike, the British

Government was well disposed towards the idea of treaty revision, and for a large part of 1946 it appears to have believed that a new agreement could, and should, be made. By August 1946, there seemed to be three difficulties, none of which appeared insuperable.[15] What should be the timing of British evacuation? Would British forces be authorised to re-enter Egypt in the event of war? And what should be the status of the Sudan?

The last question, which did not seem at first intractable, was to prove the breaking point in the Anglo-Egyptian conversations about treaty revision. The British Government view, stated in April 1946, was that it was 'aiming at a free and independent Sudan which will be able as soon as independence has been achieved to define for itself its relations with Great Britain and Egypt'. Early in 1947 the Egyptians insisted on what was called 'unity of the Nile Valley', which meant in effect annexing the Sudan to Egypt. The British Government rejected the proposal, and the Egyptian Government decided to break off negotiations.[16] From this impasse, further trouble would follow.

The end of the war was followed by more serious difficulties in Palestine. By September 1945, European Jews who had survived the Holocaust were flooding into the country, and the quota of 75,000 was within 3,000 of fulfilment.[17] The British Government was placed in a fearful dilemma. Promises to the Arabs – and, indeed, the maintenance of civil order in Palestine – prescribed that immigration should cease. But public sympathy for survivors of the Nazi genocide prescribed that it should continue – and, indeed, that it should proceed at a much faster rate. To make matters more difficult, none of the victorious Allies showed much enthusiasm for receiving substantial numbers of these tragic people in their own countries. In the United States, where a Jewish lobby was vociferous and influential, there was growing pressure for immediate acceptance of 100,000 more Jews into Palestine, and President Truman (who had succeeded Roosevelt in April) gave public support for that figure.

Britain had every reason to wish to involve other countries, most particularly the United States, in any policy that might be adopted. In November 1945, a Joint Committee was appointed by the British and American Governments to examine the problem and make recommendations. At the same time, Truman resiled from his specific demand for 100,000 immigrants.

Meanwhile, both Arabs and Jews began to prepare for the future. The Arabs of Palestine and the nearby states drew together in what became known as the Arab League. Jews began to seize arms and to smuggle large numbers of unauthorised immigrants into the country. Many arrived in unseaworthy boats, and the British authorities sought, so far as possible, to transfer them to sounder vessels and ship them to Cyprus. Among Arabs and Jews alike, there were various shades of opinion as to what policy should be adopted, and nobody was really able to speak with much authority for either community. In the pre-war period, the British authorities had been troubled mainly by violence from Arabs; but in the immediate aftermath the main violence came from Jewish extremists. The most spectacular single incident was in July 1946, when Jewish terrorists blew up the King David Hotel in Jerusalem, a building that doubled as headquarters of the government secretariat.

The Anglo-American Committee of Inquiry reported in April 1946. Many points were made in the Report; but the one that attracted most attention was the recommendation that the figure of 100,000 immigrants should be accepted immediately. This was received by the British Government with visible dismay; as Bevin told the Cabinet, the Report 'would accentuate all the existing difficulties and create much trouble with both Jews and Arabs'.[18] In the latter part of 1946 and early 1947, various possible solutions for the Palestine problems were advanced; but all of them floundered for one reason or another. In the end, the British Government resolved to refer the whole matter of Palestine to the United Nations. The Special Committee which the United Nations set up recommended partition: a proposal which was bound to involve serious trouble with both groups.

The British Government had already sought advice from its Chiefs of Staff as to whether it would be possible to enforce any policy which was opposed by both Jews and Arabs, and received the clear answer that this could not be done without substantial additions to the forces available.[19] Politically, the idea of sending many more troops to Palestine was out of the question. During the war, the British public had been willing to send soldiers to fight the recognised enemy; but no British Government could get away with a policy which would involve sending them to the Middle East for an indefinite period, where they were equally likely to be killed by Jews or Arabs. This was not unlike the situation already developing in India. So the Cabinet decided to surrender the Palestine Mandate. What might happen thereafter would be for others to decide.[20]

In May 1948, the British Mandate ended, and British troops departed from Palestine. Jews proclaimed the State of Israel, and Arabs promptly invaded from all sides, intending to destroy the new country. What ultimately emerged from the conflict was an uneasy truce, which has been repeatedly broken and remade down to our own day. Egypt was able to seize the 'Gaza Strip' in the extreme south-west of Israel. Transjordan, where the British Mandate had been relinquished two years earlier, took enough of former Palestine west of the River Jordan to justify the country renaming itself Jordan.

Here, surely, was a great paradox. Britain had accepted the Palestine Mandate essentially as a duty, not as a coveted new asset. Yet the British tenure of Palestine would prove of enormous importance in the wider story of British influence in the Middle East for many years to come. If Britain could be driven from one position, why not from others?

7
The Road to Suez

The full effect of Britain's departure from Palestine in 1948 on her whole position in the Middle East was not immediately obvious. In March 1951 Herbert Morrison, who was briefly Foreign Secretary, felt entitled to assure his Cabinet colleagues that 'the United Kingdom still commands on the whole more influence and goodwill in the Middle East than any other Foreign Power'.[1] Long before the year was out, that sanguine picture had begun to change dramatically. Within six years, British influence in the Middle East was to be damaged irretrievably.

In Britain, the late 1940s and early 1950s were a period of political instability. The Labour Party had won a huge majority in 1945, but in the later 1940s there was much reason to anticipate that this majority would be much reduced, or reversed, when another General Election took place. The General Election of February 1950 gave Labour an overall majority of only five seats. Thereafter, all kinds of vicissitudes confronted Attlee's administration. Another General Election in October 1951 resulted in this tiny Labour majority being replaced by a Conservative majority not much larger. Winston Churchill became Prime Minister for the second time, while Anthony Eden, his Foreign Secretary during most of the war years, returned to his old job.

Party attitudes to international questions were perhaps more similar than most politicians would have cared to admit, but foreign governments were encouraged to exploit the unstable situation in Britain as far as possible. Paradoxically, the Middle Eastern governments, which were far more deeply unstable, were disposed by their very instability to adopt increasingly assertive attitudes towards British interests in the hope of rallying public support against an external foe.

In July 1951, the assassination of King Abdullah of Jordan removed the closest British ally in the area. The country had recently acquired a large population from Palestine which had no tradition of loyalty to the Hashemite dynasty. Abdullah's son and immediate successor Talal was mentally ill and was soon replaced by his own young son, Hussein. Jordan became the target of intrigues from several different quarters. Astonishingly, Hussein survived them all and was still King of Jordan when he died in 1999. The immediate threat to Jordan was gradually removed, and for several years to come British influence remained.

At the other end of the Middle East, Britain was involved in considerable difficulties with Iran. In 1950, that country was still the largest oil producer in the area, running a little ahead of Saudi Arabia.[2] British interests had been of major importance in Iranian oil production from the very beginning of the twentieth century. In the spring of 1951, however, a major political crisis in Iran resulted in the accession of Dr Mohammed Mussadiq to power, and the Majlis, or Parliament, resolved to nationalise the Iranian oil industry.[3] The British Government challenged the legality of this action and sought a compromise, but the talks failed. Refining operations at Abadan ceased at the end of July. Early in October 1951 British oil personnel were expelled from Iran, and diplomatic relations between the two countries were broken. The moment for this dramatic action was chosen carefully, for it took place during the period of the British General Election campaign.

The quarrel between Britain and Iran soon proved damaging to both parties, for oil production slumped dramatically. Diplomatic relations were resumed late in 1953. Some very complex negotiations followed, involving several countries and various commercial interests. The upshot, in August 1954, was a 25-year agreement, which was a good deal less favourable to British interests than the old arrangements, but was perhaps as good as could reasonably be hoped.

Problems with Egypt proved more protracted and more serious than troubles with Iran. It is not difficult to relate these problems to the tottering authority of the country's government and its desire to make the dissipated King Farouk appear as a national champion against British imperialism. The old questions of an early revision of the Anglo-Egyptian Treaty of 1936, and a possible end to the Condominium agreement of 1899 over the Sudan, ran on. In October 1951, the Egyptian parliament passed measures purporting to abrogate both the Treaty and the Condominium agreement. The British Government denied the authority of that legislation under international law.[4] Serious anti-British rioting soon followed, to which the British replied by occupying Ismailia and Port Said. The Treaty authorising the British to be present in Egypt would expire in five years, whatever happened; but events like these suggested that the intervening period might be acrimonious.

From July 1952 onwards, Egyptian events moved rapidly. Several governments followed each other in quick succession, until General Neguib, heading a group of officers, established a clear ascendancy and King Farouk was deposed. The new government was more willing to come to terms with Britain on both outstanding issues. Early in 1953, agreement was reached on the Sudan. A Commission of five – two Sudanese, one Briton, one Egyptian and one Pakistani – would assist the Governor-General for three years, at the end of which time all foreign troops would be evacuated. The right of the Sudan to choose either independence or union with Egypt was acknowledged. A new and wider agreement with Britain emerged in October 1954, acknowledging, among other things, that British troops should evacuate all Egyptian territory within 20 months – that is, by the expiry date of the 1936 Treaty.

*

In April 1955, Winston Churchill retired from the Premiership and was succeeded by Sir Anthony Eden. The Roman historian Tacitus once declared that Nero's immediate successor Galba would have been 'by universal consent worthy to be Emperor, if he had not been Emperor'.[5] Similar remarks might be made about Eden. He had been regarded for years as Churchill's natural successor. He was held in considerable respect not only in his own party, but in both opposition parties as well. Shortly after assuming office, Eden called a new General Election and won a substantially increased majority: an achievement which was regarded in those days as very unusual. Everything seemed set for a long Eden Ministry. But this was not to be.

The events which would soon lead to the disruption of the Eden government, and which would play a major part in undermining

British authority world-wide, were complex. They occurred in many places, and some of them seemed at first to have little to do with vital British interests. Some of these developments had already begun before Eden became Prime Minister.

In Egypt, the new government which followed the deposition of Farouk began by seeking to achieve internal and external stability, and started to tackle long-overdue reforms, notably in relation to land distribution. By the end of 1954, however, Neguib had been pushed aside, and his former subordinate, Colonel Abdul Nasser, was firmly in control. At first, this change does not seem to have disturbed Britain unduly. Another important factor in the area was the growing hostility between Egypt and Israel. Although the United Nations had engineered a truce between Israel and the Arab states in 1949, neither Egypt nor the other Arab governments formally recognised the existence of Israel at all. In February 1955 a clash occurred near Gaza which was more serious than any other encounter since 1949, and tensions between Israel and Egypt continued to increase.

Far from Egypt, other important events were taking place which would also affect the general pattern in the Middle East. Before the end of 1954, the British Government had encouraged diplomatic approaches between Turkey and Iraq.[6] Early in 1955, a mutual defence agreement was made by the two countries, which became known as the Baghdad Pact. In several places, there was a desire to extend the Pact into a much more general agreement. Eden thought that it might 'grow into a NATO for the Middle East'.[7] The Pact was structured so that other countries could join, and in March 1955 Eden, still at that time the Foreign Secretary, persuaded the Cabinet to include Britain in the agreement.[8] Later in the year, Iran and Pakistan also joined the Baghdad Pact.

In other places, however, reactions to the Pact were very different. Predictably, the Soviet Union opposed it. So also did India. More immediately significant were the attitudes of Arab states. Even before Britain joined, Eden had warned his colleagues of likely opposition from Egypt, Saudi Arabia and, 'for the time being at least', Syria.[9]

Egyptian opposition may well have been founded on Nasser's concern that no other major centre of Arab influence should emerge which might rival Egypt. More surprising was the attitude of the United States, which had encouraged the parties to make the agreement, but refused to join when they did so. On this matter as on many others, President Eisenhower appears to have been following the advice of his Secretary of State, J.F. Dulles – and Dulles, in turn, seems to have been obsessed by the need to reach an agreement between Israel and the Arab states first.[10]

Then came an important development of a different kind. In September 1955, the Egyptian Government announced an agreement with Czechoslovakia, a member of the Soviet bloc, for the supply of arms. In the middle of this complex struggle over Middle Eastern power politics, the Egyptian Government began to prepare a massive engineering work, the Aswan High Dam, which was designed to control the Nile flooding and greatly increase the cultivable area of Egypt. At the turn of 1955–56 – in spite (or possibly because) of the Czechoslovak arms deal – it was made known that the United States proposed to loan $56 million, and Britain $14 million, towards the construction, and it appeared likely that the World Bank (sometimes called the International Bank) would provide $200 million.

1956 began badly for British interests in the Middle East. Early in the year, Jordan decided not to join the Baghdad Pact. Not long afterwards, King Hussein suddenly dismissed General Glubb, the British Commandant of the Jordanian army, which was usually called the Arab Legion. Eden, who had recently conceived a violent hatred of the Egyptian leader, saw the hand of Nasser in both events: 'I say he is our enemy and he shall be treated as such,' the Prime Minister declared angrily to a sceptical minister.[11]

Nasser certainly began to behave in a disturbing manner in several ways. His speeches, and Egyptian propaganda in general, were hostile to Britain. There was growing concern that Nasser's ambitions extended far beyond the boundaries of Egypt and that he sought some kind of hegemony over the whole Arab world. Doubts about Egypt's capacity to meet the proposed Aswan loan became stronger, not least because other expensive ventures of a less peaceful character were also being undertaken.

By mid-1956, leading statesmen in both the United States and Britain became very dubious about the desirability of proceeding with the Aswan Dam loan, though there was still no formal decision to abandon it. On 19 July, Secretary of State Dulles suddenly announced that the American offer would be withdrawn. This

announcement may have been precipitated by an unfortunate inter-
view between Dulles and the Egyptian Ambassador. Selwyn Lloyd,
who had become Foreign Secretary some months earlier, recorded
that the British Ambassador was informed just one hour before the
meeting at which the announcement was made, and he himself had
no idea that there was going to be an abrupt withdrawal.[12] In
Lloyd's view the real reason for Dulles's action was closely related to
questions of domestic American politics, particularly the President's
election campaign.[13] The overall effect was – again to cite Lloyd –
'just what Nasser wanted. He gained some general sympathy. He
could pretend that here was a poor country suddenly being given a
raw deal by a rich one.'[14]

On the following day the British Cabinet decided to withdraw its
offer too. So did the World Bank. The gratuitous, but perhaps unin-
tended, American snub to Britain advertised the country's weak
international status to the world. Predictably, Nasser fulminated
against Britain and America alike.

The next episode was even more dramatic. On 26 July, just a week
after cancellation of the loan, Nasser announced the 'nationalisation' of the Suez Canal. By this word he apparently meant that the
properties of the internationally-based Suez Canal Company were to
be seized and the Company's assets appropriated by the Egyptian
Government, ostensibly to defray the cost of building the dam.
British interests were particularly closely involved. Nearly a third of
the 14,666 ships which had passed through the canal in 1955 were
British.[15] Oil, rather than Imperial trade, was now the crucial factor.
More than half of the Middle Eastern oil, on which the British
economy depended, passed through the Suez Canal, and much of
the remainder went by pipeline to Levantine ports which already
were, or were likely to become, subject to Egyptian influence.[16] Thus
far, however, British ships were not stopped from passing through
the Canal.[17] Condemnation of the Egyptian action over the Suez
Canal was more or less universal in Britain. Yet the Cabinet recognised that any argument based on the allegation that Nasser had
acted illegally was of dubious force:

> The Suez Canal Company was registered as an Egyptian
> Company under Egyptian law ... Colonel Nasser had indicated
> that he intended to compensate the stakeholders at ruling market

prices. From a narrow legal point of view, his action amounted to no more than a decision to buy out the shareholders.[18]

Possible British responses were considered. Political and economic measures would certainly be applied. Egyptian sterling balances and assets, for example, were soon frozen. But what if such measures should prove inadequate? On the day after Nasser's announcement, the Cabinet agreed that 'our continued interests in the area must, if necessary, be safeguarded by military action'.[19]

Contact was immediately made with the United States and France, with a view to joint action. Dulles 'made it clear that the United States Government would strongly deprecate any premature use of force'.[20]

The three countries agreed to call an international conference of interested states, although there is little sign that the British Government was ever sanguine about its success. The conference's statement of principles was rejected by Nasser, who declared that they were 'a hostile infringement of Egypt's sovereignty'.

The next idea which emerged was to set up a Suez Canal Users' Association. Its function was not wholly clear, but it was apparently intended to 'stand ready to organise navigation, hire pilots and generally supervise the management of the Canal'.[21] Dulles, however, made it clear that American ships would not attempt to 'shoot their way' through the Canal, but would use the longer route round the Cape instead. The American insistence that force must not be used was repeated again and again during the discussions. By contrast, Harold Macmillan, Chancellor of the Exchequer, told the Cabinet that

> It was unlikely that the effective international control over the Canal could be recovered without use of force. He regarded the establishment of this users' organisation as a step towards the ultimate use of force.[22]

American opposition to force admits of several interpretations, not necessarily mutually exclusive. American interest in the Suez Canal, though strong, was a good deal less so than that of Britain. The United States was disposed to take a broader view of Nasser's action, and to see it in a more general context of world events and policies. There was also a strong American sense of 'legalism', particularly in the mind of Dulles, who was a lawyer and really does seem to have believed that an acceptable result would eventually emerge, if only proper procedures were followed. Furthermore, new Presidential and Congressional elections were approaching rapidly, and the Republican administration was laying considerable emphasis on its peaceful policies, which seemed to be evoking a sympathetic response from the electorate.

There remained another possible way of achieving a peaceful solution, which was through the United Nations. On 23 September, more than two months after seizure of the Canal, the British and French Governments appealed to the Security Council. Discussions began early in October; but any effective action was blocked by the Soviet veto.

Other international contacts were made by Britain. The French Government of Guy Mollet took an almost Apocalyptic view of the developing crisis. Early in October, Eden told the Cabinet, with evident relish, that the French

> believed that, if [Nasser's] ambitions were not checked, the political as well as the economic future of Europe would be in jeopardy. For they feared that, in that event, existing régimes in other Arab states would collapse and the Middle East would pass under the influence, not so much of Egypt, but of the Soviet Union. Europe itself would be at the mercy of the Russians.[23]

The French Ministers were certainly worried about the immediate problem of Suez nationalisation; but what concerned them most acutely was Nasser's supposed encouragement of the widespread revolt against French rule in Algeria.

Israel was also brought into the Suez negotiations, though for a very different reason. It appeared to the government of David Ben Gurion that the country's profound insecurity in the face of hostile Arab neighbours could best be relieved by some convincing demonstration of military prowess against one of them. At first, Jordan seemed a likely target, but any Israeli action against Jordan would prove disastrous for British plans. Eden explained to the Dominion Prime Ministers that Britain had a treaty under which she might find herself obliged to 'fight alongside Jordan, with Egypt as our Ally, against Israel, armed with weapons from Canada and France.

You ... will understand what a nightmare that prospect has been.'[24] Israel was gently deflected from action against Jordan, and encouraged to look instead at Egypt, which had been troubling her for some time by what were known as the 'Fedayeen' raids.[25]

Thus the governments of Britain, France and Israel all had strong, though very different, reasons to desire the destruction of Nasser, and to all of them the price of a brief war against Egypt appeared acceptable. If Egypt was defeated in such a war, Nasser would be discredited and would almost certainly fall from power. By mid-October 1956, events were moving rapidly towards a climax. Very likely the American elections, which were due on 6 November, had something to do with the timing.

On 18 October, the Cabinet was warned that matters 'might be brought rapidly to a head as a result of military action by Israel against Egypt',[26] and military preparations by Britain and France were swiftly set in place. Then there was a brief hitch in plans, and for a few days it seemed unlikely that Israel would launch a serious attack against Egypt at all.[27] Soon, however, the Prime Minister was able to reassure his colleagues on that score.

Eden envisaged that Israel would attack Egypt, whereupon the British and French would demand that both belligerents agree to withdraw to 10 miles from the Canal. If either failed to give such an undertaking, Britain and France would intervene. The Prime Minister foresaw that

> Israel might well undertake to comply ... If Egypt also complied, Colonel Nasser's prestige would be fatally undermined. If she failed to comply, there would be ample justification for Anglo-French military action against Egypt in order to safeguard the Canal.[28]

In the Cabinet discussion, some members pointed out that the demand that both parties should withdraw 10 miles from the Canal was hardly 'holding the balance'. The frontier lay a long way east of the Canal, and 'we should be asking the Egyptians to withdraw still further within their territory, while leaving the Israeli forces on Egyptian soil well in advance of their own position'. The problem of likely American responses was also raised; but, whatever reservations remained, the Cabinet agreed to act as Eden recommended, in cooperation with France.

On 29 October, Israeli forces attacked Egypt, and on the following day the agreed ultimata were sent. A further demand was slipped into the ultimatum to Egypt: that Anglo-French forces should be authorised to move into key positions at Port Said, Ismailia and Suez, to guarantee freedom of transit through the Canal. As intended, Israel accepted the demand and Egypt rejected it. On 31 October, Anglo-French aircraft bombed Egyptian airfields, to neutralise the Egyptian air force.

The United Nations swung into action, and the United States took a far more active interest in events than had apparently been expected. An American resolution to the Security Council demanding a cease-fire and criticising the attack was vetoed by Britain – an action without precedent. Early in the morning of 2 November, the General Assembly (where no veto was possible) accepted a similar resolution by 64 votes to five, with six abstentions. The five countries opposing the resolution were Britain, France, Israel, Australia and New Zealand. Among the abstentions were Canada and South Africa. The United States and the Soviet Union voted together in the majority, where they were supported by the other three Commonwealth countries which were authorised to vote: India, Pakistan and Ceylon.

By this time, the Suez crisis was disclosing profound differences of opinion in Britain and in the wider Commonwealth. Within the Conservative Party itself, the so-called 'Suez Group' had eagerly pressed for hostile action against Egypt for several months, while many members of the party took a radically different view. When the attack came, two junior ministers felt obliged to resign from the Government in protest. The Labour and Liberal Parties were incensed at the Suez episode, and on 31 October, at the end of a two-day debate, the House of Commons divided on party lines; but a Labour MP who agreed with the Government on the matter took the occasion to resign from his Party and from Parliament.

Self-governing Commonwealth countries were informed of British decisions, but were not consulted before they were taken. Their attitudes differed greatly. Robert Menzies of Australia signalled approval of the ultimatum, but even he urged Eden to 'make it your personal business to do everything possible to secure some broad basis of agreement with the United States'.[29] Eden did not intend to do anything of the kind, but did not propose to alienate Menzies by saying so. Sidney Holland of New Zealand, whose delegation also supported the Anglo-French action in the United Nations Assembly, was, in private, even less happy about it than the Australians. He told the British High Commissioner that his country, if it had been asked, would probably have recommended that the matter should be given to the Security Council.[30] The New Zealand Government was also anxious to avoid too close involvement, and requested that their cruiser *Royalist*, which was currently in the Mediterranean, should not be used in active operations.[31] In both Pacific Dominions, the opposition Parties adopted attitudes similar to their British counterparts.

Jawaharlal Nehru of India expressed a very critical view indeed: 'Instead of punishing the aggressor Israel we were punishing the victim of aggression Egypt.'[32] The same opinion was advanced by Solomon Bandaranaike of Ceylon.[33] Pakistani views were at first a trifle ambivalent. Firoz Noon, the Foreign Minister, declared, 'privately and off the record', that 'he had felt all along that a satisfactory settlement of the Suez question could not be obtained without use of force'.[34] Prime Minister Huseyn Suhrawardy, however, 'greatly regretted' the Anglo-French action, and foresaw 'calamitous consequences'.[35] Eric Louw of South Africa, whose country's delegation had abstained from voting on the General Assembly resolution, was strongly critical of the British failure to consult before issuing the ultimatum.[36]

More worrying to the British Government was the attitude of Canada, the other Commonwealth country which had abstained from voting. Lester Pearson, currently Secretary of State for External Affairs, regretted the Anglo-French decision to deliver their ultimatum while the Security Council had the matter under discussion.[37] Prime Minister Louis St Laurent warned Eden of 'the danger of a serious division within the Commonwealth ... which will prejudice the unity of our association'.[38]

In spite of the various doubts expressed by Commonwealth countries, Eden pressed ahead. The official British reply delivered to the United Nations on 3 November, was that Britain and France were ready to cease military action if and when the United Nations set up a force to intervene in the Suez Canal area, and the two belligerents agreed to accept it. This was subject to a further qualification that Egypt and Israel would both agree to accept a limited detachment of

British and French troops to be located between them until the UN forces arrived. By this time, the Israelis had pressed forward to a great military victory in Sinai.

On 5 and 6 November, Anglo-French troops were landed in the Suez area. While this was happening, the UN General Assembly carried another resolution, this time without opposing votes. The resolution, which was moved by Canada, called for the establishment of a UN force in the area within 48 hours.

The new move by Britain and France caused further tensions in the Commonwealth. In conversation with the British High Commissioner, Canadian Prime Minister St Laurent was very forthright:

> He ... spoke under obviously great emotion and indeed anger. He said that the Canadian government had been hoping that the British and French governments should not go in ... . He spoke very gravely about effect on the Commonwealth. He greatly feared that Asian members may decide to leave. That would be disastrous.[39]

That apprehension was reinforced by Suhrawardy of Pakistan, who told of messages from his country's missions abroad 'advising withdrawal from Commonwealth as only means of preserving Pakistani prestige in Middle East', a course which he personally was 'very loath' to take.[40]

When the Canadian resolution was carried by the United Nations, the Secretary-General asked the British and French Governments whether they recognised the decision as meeting their demands, indicating that – if so – he proposed to call for a cease-fire. The two countries agreed, and the cease-fire took place at midnight on 6–7 November.

One of the many distressing features of the 'Suez' fiasco was that it coincided closely with the Hungarian uprising against Soviet control, which the Russians eventually suppressed. This matter particularly exercised Louis St Laurent of Canada, who

> had hoped that Britain and France would have weighed the fact that the landing of their forces would divert the attention of the world from the tragedy of Hungary and would take the pressure

off Russia. There were those who thought that Russia had changed her mind and re-entered Hungary with overwhelming force because she calculated that British and French action gave her the opportunity to get away with it.[41]

After the cease-fire, the story of the Suez episode was largely one of damage-limitation. British and French troops finally left Suez on 22 December. The Canal itself, whose passage was a matter of immense importance to all four belligerent countries, was blocked with ships which Egypt had sunk during active hostilities. After the fighting ceased, several months of squabbling ensued before it was cleared again.

Eden's health had been precarious for some time, and perhaps that fact provides the best excuse for his often incongruous actions. Soon after the débâcle, he sought to recuperate in Jamaica and then returned to his duties. This proved too much for him, and on strong medical advice he retired from office on 9 January 1957. Ironically, Harold Macmillan, who, after Eden himself, had been the principal 'hawk' in the government, was the chosen successor.

The four countries principally involved all had good reason to count the cost. In a military sense, Israel had fared best; but the problem of hostile neighbours had not been resolved. Arab animosity was unabated and further conflict in the future was humanly certain. Egypt had won a great diplomatic victory, but she had also sustained a serious military defeat. If the main French aim had been to secure Algeria, this was a disastrous failure. Years of bloodshed followed, until the country became independent in 1962. Britain suffered as heavily, and the immense world sympathy which she enjoyed in 1945 was largely lost.

Many forecasts were disproved. Initially, Nasser gained much in prestige, and in 1958 Egypt was able to form a union with Syria, under the name of the United Arab Republic. However, no other countries joined the union and it collapsed three years later. A different Arab union had a very brief existence. In 1958, a federation was established between Britain's erstwhile clients Iraq and Jordan; but a few months later a revolt in Iraq resulted in the assassination of King Feisal and the end of his monarchy. The pro-British Nuri es-Said, who had been Prime Minister on no fewer than 14 occasions, was killed the following day.

Although fears that Pakistan, and perhaps others, would be driven to secede were not realised, Commonwealth ties were impaired by the Suez episode. While the Eden government engaged in its 'sordid conspiracy'[42] with France and Israel – as one dissident minister described it – the Commonwealth split three ways. Australia and New Zealand backed Britain in the United Nations, although they appear to have done so primarily out of a sense of loyalty to the 'Mother Country' – a loyalty which was not always properly repaid in the years which followed. Even so, New Zealand noted Britain's failure to involve other Commonwealth countries in discussions, and Australia proffered wise advice which Eden failed to take. The three Asian countries, who had no reason to feel similar loyalty, voted against Britain. Of all the Commonwealth countries, it was Canada who emerged from the crisis with her world reputation much enhanced.

Successive British governments had long regarded the Empire or Commonwealth as an institution of major world importance, in which Britain's own leadership was entrenched and permanent. They were disposed to inform Commonwealth countries what Britain proposed to do, but not to consult them before the policy was decided. The opportunity to evolve a policy which would have been generally acceptable to the Commonwealth as a whole was missed. If the attempt had been made, there can be little doubt that this would have proved of great benefit both to the Commonwealth and to Britain herself.

8
Colonial Africa

After the spate of 'decolonisation' in Asia in the late 1940s, the remainder of the British Empire seemed to have settled into a phase of modest advance in the direction of eventual, but distant, independence. The next important period of radical change affected Africa.

In 1945, a great deal of the continent formed part of the British Empire. The territories were of several different kinds. The Union of South Africa was a fully self-governing Dominion, with the acknowledged right to secede from the Empire when and if it chose to do so. Other places ranked as Colonies in the strict sense of the term, over which the United Kingdom had ultimate control, but which had limited and revocable powers of self-government, varying widely from place to place. There were also Protectorates, in which local rulers exercised considerable powers. In addition, there were Mandates, former German colonies held under authority of the now moribund League of Nations, to which, in theory at least, Britain was responsible. When the United Nations was fully established, most Mandates became UN Trust Territories.

The process of withdrawal from the many British dependencies in Africa followed different patterns in different places; but the main changes which excited world interest occurred in a very short period in the late 1950s and early 1960s. There are parallels with the process of imperial withdrawal from Asia a decade or so earlier; but there are also some very sharp differences.

For a long time, official British attitudes to people living in colonial territories had been strongly paternalist. This was illustrated by a controversy over Kenya early in the 1920s. The population of the colony was overwhelmingly African, but there were also many Indians and considerable numbers of Europeans who wished to remain there. The Colonial Governor, Major-General Sir Edward Northey, who was anxious to encourage the immigration of British ex-servicemen and their families, had unwisely asserted that 'European interests must be paramount'. But Northey soon departed and his view was emphatically confuted in a Government White Paper of 1923, which asserted 'that the interests of the African natives must be paramount and that if, and when, these interests and the interests of the immigrant races should conflict, the former should prevail'.[1] This statement was not made by any sort of radical, but appeared with the authority of the 9th Duke of Devonshire, Colonial Secretary in Bonar Law's Conservative Government. There was genuine concern for the well-being of 'natives' in all colonies; but at that stage nobody contemplated that they would come to form the principal element in the government of the colony for a very long time to come.

During the inter-war period, ideas developed considerably. Industrial and trading organisations in Africa began to look more like their British counterparts, and workers expressed their griev-ances through strikes. The view that colonies must eventually become self-governing territories became increasingly general. The wartime Coalition Government, and – for some time – the post-war Labour Government seemed willing to continue this policy.[2] As time went on, substantial constitutional changes were made in many places, designed to give colonial peoples a greater share in the government of their countries. These, however, were essentially responses to developments within individual Colonies.

In 1949, Colonial Secretary Creech Jones drew his colleagues' atten-tion to the fact that constitutional developments had hitherto been the result of 'ad hoc decisions without reference to an accepted body of principles'.[3] There was general agreement that a comprehensive enquiry was necessary. The consequences were not immediate, and for some time there was little indication that most of the African depen-dencies would become independent in the near future. But in the course of the 1950s, several quite different developments took place, all of which were important in the great colonial changes which followed.

First of these was the rise of 'African nationalism'. Although it had been clear for years that many of the colonies would eventually become self-governing, it was by no means equally clear what form their self-government would take, or when it was likely to occur. The process of changing African colonies into independent countries posed problems which were markedly different from those which had been faced in the most important Asian possessions. Most of the colonial boundaries in Africa had been fixed within the previous 60 or 70 years. Those boundaries had been drawn by European Powers for their own convenience. They linked African groups who had nothing in common; they cut across traditional African societies. Could European administrative units created almost or quite within living memory ever be turned into viable African nations? Most African nationalists decided that this could be done and sought to act on that assumption.

Many Britons (including enlightened Britons who had no sympathy whatever with racist views) were disposed to view African nationalism with suspicion. When only a small proportion of the black population of an African colony had received the education and training which were considered necessary for administration of a modern state, was it in the true interest of the African majority to relinquish control of that country quickly? Would this mean, in practice, shifting power from an experienced and impartial European élite to an African élite which was neither experienced nor impartial? But in the post-war period nationalism grew at an ever-increasing pace. No ambitious African politician could allow others to outbid him in the clamour for change. At the same time, politicians were constantly watching what was happening in other territories. If, for example, the Gold Coast was moving swiftly towards independence, could Nigeria hold back, even though there were very important factors at work which suggested that it might be in the best interests of her peoples to develop at a slower pace?

The second important development was the eclipse of Britain's world power, partly as a result of wartime changes and partly as a result of Suez. The fact that the most spectacular changes in Britain's imperial rôle in Africa took place in the decade after Suez is only partly a coincidence.

Another factor, difficult to quantify but probably very important, was the changing British view of the profitability of Empire. In the period of massive imperial expansion which marked the late nineteenth century, there were voices which contended that Empire was a burden rather than an asset; but such voices were drowned in the popular clamour. It later began to dawn on many people that these sceptics might be right. One recent writer has observed, with a measure of exaggeration, that 'up to the Second World War, Britain's vast African estate had proved of negligible value, despite the mytho-logical treasure chest believed to be buried there'.[4] After 1945, much new evidence upheld the sceptics' view. Partly, no doubt, this was the result of decisions by many countries, often acting through the General Agreement on Tariffs and Trade (GATT), to liberalise trade, which reduced the perceived need for captive markets and sources of raw materials. Again, for whatever reason, withdrawal from India and the other rich Asian possessions had not been accompanied by any downswing in British domestic prosperity. Early evidence from Africa suggested that the same thing would happen there.

Down to the early 1950s, people who advocated advances towards colonial independence were conscious that the burden of proof lay on their shoulders. By 1955, however, matters had changed very considerably. In February of that year, a significant paper was circu-lated to the Cabinet by Lord Swinton, Secretary of State for Commonwealth Relations. The office over which he presided was concerned mainly with self-governing Commonwealth countries, but its interests sometimes overlapped with those of the Colonial Office. The draft of Swinton's paper had been circulated to leading Canadian, Australian and New Zealand statesmen, who concurred with his findings. All agreed that the long-established policy

> of assisting dependent peoples to reach a stage of development where they can assume responsibility for managing their own affairs ... cannot now be halted or reversed, and it is only to a limited extent that its pace can be controlled by the United Kingdom government ... . In the main, the pace of constitutional change will be determined by the strength of nationalist feeling and the development of political consciousness within the terri-tories concerned.[5]

Traditionally, the Conservatives had been seen by friends and foes alike as the 'party of Empire', and it is one of the great paradoxes of British politics that the 13 years of Conservative rule from 1951 to

1964 were to witness a massive, and largely a deliberate, retreat from Empire. The first Colonial Secretary of the period was Oliver Lyttleton, who clearly visualised an orderly and gradual process towards self-government, probably extending over many years. His successor Alan Lennox-Boyd, who held office from 1954 to 1959, had a long-term and deep interest in colonial affairs, and his views were probably similar to those of Lyttleton. His policy, however, was thrown seriously off course by events not of his making. Suez and its aftermath were bad enough; but the growing disposition of other imperial Powers, most notably France, to withdraw precipitately from their own empires made it very difficult for Britain to act in a radically different way. Then, towards the end of the decade, the Macmillan Government began to show an increasing interest in European rather than imperial links (even though Britain's formal application for membership of the European Economic Community did not take place until two years after Lennox-Boyd left office). By the time of his departure in 1959, immediately after his party won an increased majority at the polls, he was probably glad to go.

Iain Macleod, who succeeded Lennox-Boyd, was widely regarded as a political 'whiz kid', for whom the Colonial Office was but a staging post. Macleod was convinced that the process of colonial independence in Africa must be accelerated, or there would be 'terrible bloodshed'.[6] At first strongly supported by Prime Minister Harold Macmillan, Macleod later fell foul of the 'right' of his party. In 1961, Macleod moved to a different Cabinet post. The two years in which Macleod was Colonial Secretary are considered by some[7] to have been the 'decisive years' in the process; but we have seen strong evidence that it was already running out of control some years earlier. Macleod's two Conservative successors, Reginald Maudling and Duncan Sandys, both had important careers ahead of them in other fields, but do not seem to have left a great mark on colonial policy. Certainly by the autumn of 1961, and perhaps long before, the lines had been indelibly drawn.

The Gold Coast, now Ghana, proved to be the front runner in the dramatic change which soon took place. Like many colonies, it was under control of a Governor, assisted by Executive and Legislative Councils.[8] The British part of Togoland, held originally as a League of Nations Mandate, and later as a UN Trust Territory, was for many purposes treated as part of the Gold Coast. In 1946, a new constitution was granted, which gave elected members of the Legislative Council a substantial majority over all other members combined. The change was enthusiastically welcomed by the local people; but in the next couple of years serious economic troubles arose.

Early in 1948, there were major riots in Accra and other towns, resulting in 29 deaths and many more injuries. A committee of inquiry recognised various causes, including the consequences of African soldiers returning from service in the Forces, frustration among educated Africans who saw no prospect of political power, increasing contacts with political developments elsewhere, and failure of the British Government to take measure of the spread of literacy and the growing importance of liberal ideas.[9] These disturbances were followed by widespread demands for further constitutional reforms, which were soon granted. A new movement, the Convention People's Party (CPP), headed by Kwame Nkrumah, rapidly emerged as the spearhead of demands for more change still, and a campaign of boycotts and strikes began. Nkrumah was arrested; but in 1951, when the first Legislative Council elections were held under a more democratic system, the CPP won a large majority of those seats whose representatives were chosen by popular election. Nkrumah was released, and a struggle developed between the CPP and those Legislative Council members who had been chosen by the State Councils, in which traditional chiefs played a major role.

Meanwhile, a remarkably close cooperation developed between Nkrumah and the Governor of the Gold Coast, Sir Charles Arden-Clarke. But there were serious difficulties about public attitudes to constitutional development, particularly in the central and northern areas. The British Government insisted that the final stages of an advance towards independence should not take place until another General Election was held and a reasonable majority of the new legislature confirmed that it supported these steps. Further elections in July 1956 gave the CPP a substantial overall majority, and when the new legislature met a motion calling for independence was carried without opposition. Even so, at least one member of the British Cabinet expressed doubt whether it was right to go ahead, arguing that it would place 'tribal inhabitants of the Central and Northern territories ... under the control of the more advanced and educated merchant groups of the industrial areas'.[10] Despite such qualms, the Government went ahead.

There was also a special problem with the British section of Togoland. The Ewe people who lived there extended also into French Togoland, and there was some local pressure against incorporation into an independent Gold Coast. In a plebiscite of May 1956, however, a majority accepted continuance of the association, and this view was later accepted by the United Nations.

The British Government accepted the general verdict of the people of the Gold Coast and Togoland, and in March 1957 the country – now renamed Ghana – received independence. The change from colonial status had taken place rapidly, and, on the whole, remarkably peacefully. At the Conference of Commonwealth Prime Ministers a couple of months later, Ghana was accepted as full member of the Commonwealth. It is noteworthy that the change of status took place without opposition from any of the 'members'. These included South Africa, whose racist policies were already causing great concern in many places.

Acceptance of Ghana drew attention to the new meaning which the expression 'member of the Commonwealth' was coming to acquire. It was no longer a synonym for 'a country belonging to the British Empire'. A Cabinet memorandum of April 1953 defined a 'member of the Commonwealth' as

> a sovereign independent country, recognised as a separate international entity, but associated with other Commonwealth countries of the same status in a relationship differing from that existing between foreign States ... for practical purposes the hallmark of membership is the right to be represented at meetings of Commonwealth Prime Ministers.[11]

With some subtlety, it was acknowledged that 'the Colonies are part of the Commonwealth, but do not enjoy the status of "Members"'.

Three years after independence, Ghana followed the Indian precedent and became a Republic within the Commonwealth. This decision set up a precedent of its own, which was eventually followed by most former African colonies. Becoming a Republic rather than a 'Dominion' (or 'Realm', as these countries were sometimes called), was, in form, little more than a rather minor constitutional adjustment; but in practice the Commonwealth Republics were usually less disposed to cooperate closely with Britain in international and defence matters than were the traditional 'Dominions'. Very often, the act of becoming a Republic seems to have been inspired much more by the desire of local politicians to establish a powerful executive, untrammelled by overmuch concern for the Rule of Law, than by any idealistic quest for a more perfect democracy.

If one African country with an overwhelmingly black population could be accepted as a fully independent Commonwealth member, it was certain that others would soon follow, even though conditions were very different. In December 1958, General de Gaulle offered the choice of autonomy or full independence to the French colonies in Africa, which gave further impetus to the process.[12]

The population of Nigeria was around 31 million in 1955, compared with Ghana's 4.4 million. As with Ghana, there had been loss of life in civil disturbances of the late 1940s. The two colonies also witnessed several attempts at constitutional change during the late 1940s and early 1950s. The sharpest difference between them lay in the mixture of political, religious and tribal elements. In Ghana, considerable regional differences certainly existed, but these were not deep enough to prevent one party, the CPP, from emerging by the mid-1950s as the dominant political force in the country as a whole.

In Nigeria, by contrast, no single political movement enjoyed widespread support throughout the country. Thus, at the elections of 1954, the Northern People's Congress (NPC) was hugely predominant in the largely Hausa – and Muslim – areas of the north. In the largely Ibo eastern region, the National Council of Nigeria and the Cameroons (NCNC) led. In the mainly Yoruba western region, the NCNC and the Action Group (AG) both received substantial support; while in the southern part of the once-German Cameroons, the Kamerun National Congress (KNC) won every seat. The issues between the Nigerian political parties tended to be religious and tribal, unlike the economic and social questions which usually dominate the politics of Britain and other Western European countries.

In the first half of the 1950s, a strong argument existed for the view that, whether or not the Gold Coast was almost ready for full independence, similar developments in Nigeria would lead to disruption of the country and perhaps civil war. In 1952 and 1953, the Governor of Nigeria, Sir J. Macpherson, began to send missives to British officials, warning them that acceptance of current demands in the Gold Coast would have dire effects in his own colony.[13]

Events underlined the significance of this warning. In 1953, there was a major political crisis in the eastern region, while in the same year there was a riot in the northern town of Kano, between Hausas on one side and Ibo and Yoruba on the other, in which more than 36 people were killed. No doubt Nigerian independence would come in the end; but such events were symptomatic of a wide and general unease.

The British Government, which had made up its mind that Nigeria must advance towards independence as rapidly as possible, sought actively to resolve the issues between the regions. After a series of meetings, Oliver Lyttleton was able to announce 'unqualified success' in February 1954, and revised constitutional instruments were prepared, giving Nigeria a federal structure. In 1957 the Eastern and Western regions became self-governing, and two years later the Northern region followed.

Before this process of establishment of regional governments was complete, the British Government was compelled to consider what the next stage would be. As the Cabinet was told:

> the government were now faced with a difficult choice. Either they must concede independence too soon and risk the disinte- gration of Nigeria and a crucial breakdown of administration; or they must seek to delay the grant of independence [which] would provoke increasing animosity and disturbance.[14]

There were further complications. The Government of South Africa was 'inclined to question the right of the United Kingdom to promote colonial territories to independent status within the Commonwealth without the consent of the other self-governing members', while the Governments of Australia and New Zealand expressed 'concern about the increase in the coloured members of the Commonwealth [and the] risk that they might ultimately out- number the other members'.[15] How far members of the British Government echoed that concern was not made clear.

The British Government decided that action should be deferred until new Nigerian elections took place in 1959. But pressure for independence grew too rapidly. In August 1958 the Federal House of Representatives called, without a division, for independence by 1960. A further constitutional conference was held in London in the autumn, and accepted the proposal. On that basis the British Government complied, and arrangements were made for Nigeria to become an independent state and a full member of the British Commonwealth at the end of September 1960. In 1963, Nigeria elected to become a Republic within the Commonwealth.

At the time of Nigeria's independence, the fate of the British slice of the adjacent Cameroons remained undecided. By that date, the eastern part of the former German colony, once administered by France, had become an independent republic. In 1961 the British part of the Cameroons was invited to choose between membership of the Nigerian Federation and membership of the Cameroons Republic. The north, which had long been linked with the northern region of Nigeria for many purposes, chose to continue as a member of the Federation, while the south decided, by a more than two to one majority, to join the Cameroons Republic.

The third important British possession in West Africa was Sierra Leone, with a population of around 2.25 million in the 1950s. The original colony had been acquired as far back as 1788 as a settlement for freed slaves; but a Protectorate was declared over a much more extensive area in 1896. From the 1920s onwards, the extraction of minerals, including diamonds, iron and platinum, became a very important feature of the economy. As in Ghana and Nigeria, there was rapid advance towards self-government in the late 1940s and the 1950s.

In Sierra Leone, as in other parts of West Africa, there were various cross-currents which affected constitutional development. There were divisions between the Creoles, largely descendants of freed slaves, and the rural population.[16] The constitution of 1947, which gave a majority on the Legislative Council to elected representatives, was opposed strenuously in some quarters because it meant transferring power from the old colony to the wider protectorate. Further constitutional changes in 1951 were followed by elections in which – as in the Gold Coast – a single political party emerged as clear leader of the independence movement. In 1955, there were two phases of serious rioting, each with mainly economic causes, though the authority of traditional chiefs was also involved. The move towards independence proceeded rapidly nevertheless. Constitutional changes in 1958 resulted in virtual self-determination for internal affairs. A Constitutional Conference in

1960 agreed that Sierra Leone should receive independence in April 1961. Ten years later, Sierra Leone became a Republic within the Commonwealth.

The remaining British colony in West Africa was Gambia, a strip of territory nowhere more than 20 miles wide, thrust into the French colony of Senegal. It had virtually no minerals or manufactures. The Colonial Secretary reported that '65,000 tons of groundnuts are its only support'. Its population of around 250,000 was racially the same as that in contiguous parts of Senegal. For a long time, Gambia seemed uninterested in becoming a self-governing democracy.[17] Nevertheless, constitutional changes were introduced in 1946, and again in 1951, designed to provide, and then to extend, elected representation on the Legislative Council. Further changes followed, leading eventually to a new constitution in 1959, under which a majority of the legislature was directly elected with universal suffrage.

Early in 1961, the British Cabinet decided that it was in the interest of Gambia to establish 'some form of association with Senegal'.[18] In the following year, independence was promised as soon as negotiations with Senegal were complete.[19] But plans for an early union with Senegal miscarried. The reasons are complex;[20] but two principal explanations emerge. Culturally, Gambia is English, and Senegal is French; while chiefs, professional people and farmers in Gambia feared that amalgamation would mean absorption in a larger entity, in which their own interests would be swamped. And so, in 1965, Gambia received independence, becoming a Republic within the Commonwealth five years later.

*

In West Africa, the retreating colonial authorities were mainly concerned with the problems of indigenous peoples, for there were few immigrants who wished to settle there. In colonies in other parts of Africa, problems were compounded by the presence of substantial numbers of settlers who wished to make the colony their permanent home. Sometimes there were two or more groups of immigrants, with histories of mutual animosity.

The most important British possessions in East Africa formed a bloc of four territories: Kenya, Uganda, Tanganyika and Zanzibar.

They did not all stand in the same relationship with Britain. Kenya, originally a protectorate, became a colony in 1920. Uganda and Zanzibar had both been protectorates since the 1890s. Tanganyika had formed the largest part of German East Africa until the 1914 war. The German colony was divided by the peace treaties into Rwanda and Urundi, which were given to Belgium, and Tanganyika, which became a British Mandate under the League of Nations, and eventually a Trust Territory under the United Nations.

The fate of Kenya would attract particular attention. As in other places, the historical background was highly relevant to the problems which had to be faced in the period of imperial retreat. In the 1890s, Britain began to construct a railway linking the port of Mombasa to Lake Victoria. Neither Africans nor Europeans were eager to engage in the work, and Indians were recruited. Some remained as traders, and many other Indian traders followed. An area of highlands near Nairobi, with a mild climate, was appropriated for white settlement before 1914, and in the immediate aftermath of the war many British ex-servicemen were settled there.

For a long time to come, Kenya was generally at peace, although the country encountered considerable economic problems in the inter-war period. Down to 1951, everything seemed to point towards developments in the direction of self-government not dissimilar to those which were taking place at the other side of the continent. Then, suddenly, in the latter part of 1952, world attention was focused on the Kikuyu tribe, a Kikuyu-dominated movement known as the Kenya African Union, the KAU's leader Jomo Kenyatta, and a secret society known as Mau Mau, which was supported almost exclusively by Kikuyu.

The Kikuyu were the largest single African tribe in Kenya, but only amounted to about 30 per cent of the African population. At one time they had occupied a large part of the colony, including the 'White Highlands', but their numbers were greatly depleted in the late nineteenth century through smallpox, while their cattle were visited by rinderpest. Thus the white immigrants moved into a largely depopulated land. It is all too easy today to understand on the one hand the whites' argument that their hard work had made the land prosperous, and on the other hand the argument of many Kikuyu that the whites had encroached on their ancestral land, and permitted the indigenous people to remain there only as landless workers.

The KAU was an African self-government movement, comparable with those in West Africa. But Mau Mau was a very different matter. Members were bound together by blood-curdling initiation oaths, and in 1950 the movement was proscribed. At the end of September 1952, a campaign of Mau Mau violence began with arson and attacks on cattle. This was followed swiftly by assassination of their major Kikuyu opponent. Attacks on European settlers followed and a State of Emergency was declared. Several KAU leaders, including Kenyatta, were arrested. After long delays, the KAU leaders were convicted and imprisoned – many people now consider unjustly.

The main operational phase of the Emergency lasted until October 1956, but the Emergency was not formally ended until January 1960. It was different from most 'wars of national libera-tion' in two ways. The rebels were almost exclusively members of the Kikuyu tribe. The object of the insurrection was not so much to secure a different political system in Kenya as to drive European and Asian immigrants from the country altogether. In the end, Mau Mau was beaten, but at heavy cost.

Public attention in Britain was focused largely on the Europeans who were killed, sometimes in circumstances of particular horror. Numerically, however, Europeans formed only a tiny minority of the casualties on either side. Official figures given in June 1959[21] showed that in the period 1952–58, 1,879 civilians had been killed, of whom 1,821 were Africans, 32 Europeans and 26 Asians; 591 members of the security forces lost their lives: 525 Africans, 63 Europeans and three Asians. Mau Mau casualties were vastly greater. Over the same period, 10,540 were killed and 31,429 cap-tured. Later information has caused some of these figures to be revised, but has not altered the overall picture. Not all the violence was on one side. In the notorious Hola incident of 1959, a group of detainees, most but not all of them Mau Mau members, refused to work and were assaulted by African warders. There were savage beat-ings, and eleven people were killed.

Even during the Emergency, the process of constitutional develop-ment continued, although the process was somewhat slower than in much of West Africa. A Representative Council, which included one Indian, one Muslim and one African, was set up in 1954. In July 1959, the colonial government authorised the establishment of political parties provided that they were not racial in character, and in October of that year the British Government published policy proposals which included the equal rights of peoples of all races to acquire land in the 'White Highlands'. The end of the Emergency was followed swiftly by announcement of plans for a much broader Legislative Council. The first elections were held early in 1961, and a few weeks later a new government was set up. Thereafter matters were largely held up until August, when Jomo Kenyatta was at last released. Further talks began towards the end of 1961. It was clear, however, that considerable difficulties remained. Not only the European settlers, but the minority tribes in Kenya as well, were apprehensive of Kikuyu domination.[22] Two major political parties had emerged: Kenya African National Union (KANU), which favoured a centralised government, and Kenya African Democratic Union (KADU), which favoured a decentralised, federal structure. At one point, a complete breakdown in the talks was feared; but in the end the outlines of a new constitution were agreed – though it still proved impossible to persuade the two parties to form an interim coalition.[23]

Elections later in 1962 gave KANU a substantial majority, and pressure was generated for further government centralisation. This created a very dangerous situation. If KANU's demands were resisted, the Kenya Government might declare independence unilaterally, and it would be impossible to hold the country by force; if the demands were accepted, KADU supporters might well resort to violence. In the end, KANU proved more moderate in its demands than some had feared, and both dangers were averted.

There remained a problem of a different kind. Although Mau Mau had been defeated, the Kikuyu complaint about white people holding much of the best land was unresolved. In March 1962, Colonial Secretary Reginald Maudling told his Cabinet colleagues that the problem of landless Africans 'presented the gravest threat to security'. To meet this danger, it would be necessary to purchase European farms and equip them for African use.[24] A few months later, the Cabinet approved of plans to acquire 1 million acres of mixed farming land currently held by Europeans, over a period of five years, for the settlement of 70,000 African families, at a cost of £16.55 million.[25] The Kikuyu, however, were impatient for quicker results, and late in 1963 the Cabinet was told of the invasion of farms by landless Kikuyu with 'thefts of stock, destruction of fencing and attacks on property'.[26] This situation was met by assistance to the Kenya Government for the immediate purchase of 350,000 acres.

More constitutional talks in 1963 resulted in general agreement that Kenya should become an independent state within the Commonwealth on 12 December. Predictably, Kenyatta became the first Prime Minister. The necessary legislation encountered no difficulty in Parliament. A year later, Kenya was declared a Republic, but remained a Commonwealth member. Kenyatta became President, and continued in that office until his death in 1978.

In contiguous Uganda, problems of the 'decolonisation' period were markedly different from those in Kenya. Africans were included in the Uganda Executive Council in mid-1952, and the Legislative Council was enlarged in the following year. Uganda was affected, though only to a minor extent, by Mau Mau problems, because some Kikuyu extended beyond Kenya into Uganda.[27]

Ethnic problems were different from those in Kenya. Early in the twentieth century, there had been some white settlement, in connection with the production of coffee, cotton and rubber; but the indigenous population proved so successful in handling the business that the numbers of whites remaining during the decolonisation period were far less than in Kenya. As in Kenya, however, there were many immigrants of Indian extraction, largely traders and their families.

The most acute and immediate ethnic problems in Uganda were concerned not with these fairly recent immigrants, but with the indigenous African peoples, who numbered rather more than five million in the 1950s. The Baganda – that is, the people of Buganda, the region to the north-west of Lake Victoria – were the largest single group. They accounted for about a quarter of the population of Uganda, and presented special problems. Many had been converted to Catholic Christianity before British political influence began, but the ruling minority were Protestants. British influence in Uganda developed rapidly in the 1890s, with the Baganda acting largely as agents of that influence. In 1900, a treaty was concluded by which Buganda accepted British protection, though the country was still largely administered by its own king, the Kabaka. The behaviour of the Baganda towards other tribes during that period caused deep resentment, which was still strong in the mid-twentieth century.

Economically and politically, the Baganda were ahead of most other peoples in Uganda, and it was in Buganda that serious rioting, with anti-colonial overtones, took place in the later 1940s. It was in Buganda, too, that the first significant nationalist movement, the Uganda National Congress, appeared in 1952.

In the following year, a remarkable crisis developed in Buganda. The British Government was already convinced that decolonisation was necessary. In the middle of 1953, the Colonial Secretary delivered a speech in which he suggested rather tentatively that a Federation might be formed to cover the territories of British East Africa. Mutesa II, Kabaka of Buganda, voiced widespread local opposition to the idea, calling for separation of his kingdom from the rest of Uganda and eventual independence as a separate member of the Commonwealth. The British Government reacted sharply, withdrawing recognition of Mutesa, removing him from the country and declaring a State of Emergency in Buganda. A long wrangle began, but eventually a compromise solution was reached. It was perceived that popular support for the Kabaka was strong, and in October 1955 he was allowed to return.

Meanwhile, Uganda was moving rapidly towards independence. Political parties began to appear, split and merge in a bewildering manner; but in these parties old lines of cleavage – Baganda *versus* non-Baganda; Catholic *versus* Protestant – could often be seen. In 1958, most of the Baganda shunned the first direct Ugandan elections, and two years later the Lukiko, or Bugandan parliament, called for secession from Uganda.

In a memorandum of May 1960, Macleod seemed almost mystified about events in Uganda:

The problem here is an extremely complex and difficult one. In no other territory is the political picture so confused. No national African leader of any sort has yet emerged. In consequence the struggle goes on between the traditional forces represented by the Kabaka and the other Agreement Rulers and the rising power of the political parties. We must try to keep a balance between them and not sacrifice either ...[28]

Eventually, however, matters began to resolve themselves. When a General Election was held with universal franchise in the spring of

1961, the Baganda were exhorted by their government not to register as electors; but in Uganda as a whole sufficient people did vote
to allow a government to be formed, with a substantial majority of
posts held by Africans.

Later in 1961, proposals for a new Ugandan constitution were drawn
up at a conference in London. Uganda was to be a democratic state
with a strong central government; but Buganda was to stand in a
federal relationship with the centre, and some other tribes would also
receive special treatment. There was argument over constitutional
arrangements for some of the smaller tribes, but separatists in Buganda
were more or less mollified. So Uganda received full internal self-
government in March 1962. Another General Election followed
swiftly, as a result of which the Uganda People's Congress emerged as
the largest single party, and its leader Milton Obote was able to form a
government. After further constitutional adjustments, the British
Parliament approved the country's independence without opposition,
and Uganda was acknowledged as an independent country within the
British Commonwealth in October 1962, with Obote as Prime
Minister, but with the Queen still recognised as Head of State.

This condition did not continue for long. A year later, Uganda
was declared an 'independent sovereign state which shall cease to
form part of Her Majesty's dominions'. The word 'Republic' was
deliberately avoided, because of the monarchist proclivities of many
Ugandans, and the country remained in the Commonwealth. The
Kabaka of Buganda was chosen as the first President: a reconciliation
of traditional and modern interests.[29]

Tanganyika, and the offshore islands Unguja and Pemba which
constituted Zanzibar, had long been linked. In earlier times, the
Tanganyika coast and the islands had been much affected by Arabs,
by Shirazi (who were of Persian origin), and also by Portuguese. In
the mid-nineteenth century, Zanzibar became a major producer of
cloves from Arab-owned slave plantations. Later in the century,
arrangements made with and between the British and German
Governments resulted in Zanzibar becoming a British Protectorate –
in which slavery was soon abolished – while Tanganyika constituted
the major portion of German East Africa.[30] After the 1914–18 war,
Tanganyika became a British Mandate under the League of Nations.
At that time, there were rather more than four million Africans,
around 15,000 Asians and some 2,500 Europeans. In Zanzibar,

Africans formed nearly 80 per cent of the population, but the Protectorate was ruled, in name at least, by an Arab Sultan. The highest layer of administration was filled mainly by Europeans, the next by Arabs and the lowest by Indians.

During the inter-war period, development in Zanzibar was slow. In Tanganyika, the British sought, in principle, to work towards African self-government, but in practice they built on existing institutions, in which the rulers' attitudes tended to be conservative. No African was nominated to the Legislative Council until 1945, and none received Departmental charge until long after that.[31] Economic development was rather faster. Large-scale production came to be dominated by Europeans and Indians, while Africans developed smaller-scale agricultural production.

Soon after the end of the Second World War, a ten-year plan for development of food oil production in Tanganyika was launched. This, the 'Tanganyika ground-nut scheme', proved an economic failure and became a political *cause célèbre* in Britain. Meanwhile, ambitious Africans found themselves blocked in the central administration by Indians and whites, and in the local administration by chiefs, while their progress in commerce was impeded by the established hierarchy.

An African organisation aiming at self-government developed under the leadership of Julius Nyerere, and in 1954 took the name Tanganyika African National Union, or TANU. In 1958–59, the first elections for the Legislative Council of Tanganyika were held. The franchise was very narrow, but every one of the 30 available seats was won by TANU, or by TANU-supported candidates. The franchise was then greatly extended, though still confined to a minority. In 1960, elections were held under the new arrangements. TANU captured all but one of the seats and could fairly claim to have general support among people of all ethnic groups. Macleod regarded Tanganyika as 'the brightest spot' in East Africa:

> Julius Nyerere will be the Chief Minister. He has always shown excellent cooperation with us and the Governor and has a complete understanding of the economic needs of his country and the need for keeping British administration and know-how.[32]

Steps were soon taken towards independence. In May 1961, self-government was granted, and in December the country became fully independent. In the following year, it became a Republic within the Commonwealth, with Nyerere as President.

Events in Zanzibar took a very different course in the rapid march towards independence. Political parties began to appear in the mid-1950s and were divided essentially on ethnic lines. The first Legislative Council contests, in 1957, resulted in most seats going to Africans. Then the Council was enlarged, and in January 1961 the result was a dead heat. In the hope of breaking the deadlock, a further seat was added and another election was called in June of the same year. There was a week of large-scale rioting, order being eventually restored by the King's African Rifles. Sixty-eight people were killed, close on 400 wounded. As for the election results, these were, if anything, even less satisfactory than on the previous occasion. The African group won most of the votes, the other won most of the seats. A Constitutional Conference in the spring of 1962 failed to reach any agreement about future development.[33]

Even though the country seemed destined for an indefinite run of ethnic violence, the British Parliament decided to give Zanzibar independence. In June 1963, internal self-government was granted, and the number of seats on the Legislative Council increased to 31. Elections in the following year gave a coalition of Arab and Shirazi groups a substantial majority of seats while – again – the Africans, with a minority of seats, secured more votes. In these unpropitious conditions, full independence was granted in December. In the following month, there was a revolution in Zanzibar, associated with much violence and looting. A new and politically radical régime, headed by Abeid Karuma, took office. In the aftermath, many Arabs and Indians fled the country.

Early in April 1964, the British Cabinet heard gloomy news that Zanzibar 'was falling under the influence of the Sino-Soviet bloc'.[34] Then an astonishing new development took place. In April, Karuma met Nyerere of Tanganyika and they signed an agreement to unite the two countries. The arrangement was quickly ratified by the Tanganyika National Assembly and the Revolutionary Council of Zanzibar. The country which emerged from the union was soon renamed Tanzania.

British Somaliland presented problems of a different kind. The Somalis ranged over a large area in the vicinity of the Horn of Africa, extending into territory which today covers not only

Somalia, but also parts of several contiguous countries. In the late nineteenth century, Britain, Italy and France all acquired protectorates in the Somali region.[35] In 1940, Italian troops occupied British Somaliland, but they were driven out in the following year, and Italian Somaliland was itself soon taken by the Allies. The peace treaty with Italy after the war required all Italian colonies to be relinquished, but it was by no means clear what was to happen to them. Late in 1949, the United Nations eventually decided that Italian Somaliland, now renamed Somalia, should be administered by Italy for ten years, under UN tutelage. As for contiguous British Somaliland, the principle had long been accepted that the territory should eventually become independent, though no date had been fixed. What link, if any, should be made with Somalia was an open question.

In 1956, however, the British Government announced that representative institutions were to be introduced, as a step towards self-government, and that eventual union with Somalia would not be opposed if the people concerned so desired. New constitutional arrangements were made, and several seats on the Legislative Council of the Protectorate were to be open for popular election. In March 1959, the first elections resulted in the return of candidates who all seemed to agree on the immediate aims of independence and union with Somalia. Further constitutional changes followed, and more elections were held in February 1960 with similar results.

The last phase took place with speed which was exceptional even in the history of the British retreat from empire. At the end of 1959, the UN General Assembly had adopted a resolution to the effect that the Italian trusteeship of Somalia should end on 1 July 1960. In April, a meeting of Somalis from both the Trust Territory and the Protectorate met at Mogadishu, and called for the establishment of a unitary, democratic, parliamentary republic as soon as the trusteeship ended. The British exceeded this tight schedule by a few days, declaring the Protectorate fully independent on 26 June. All ideas of a tenuous Commonwealth link were quietly abandoned, and on 1 July the two legislatures united, becoming the National Assembly of the new Republic.

At the fringe of Empire lay the Anglo-Egyptian condominium of the Sudan. From the start, its status was ambiguous, and in practice the country was largely run as a British protectorate – though (as has been seen) Egyptian Governments sometimes laid claim to it. In so far as Britain was interested in the Sudan in the middle years of the twentieth century, that interest was essentially strategic rather than economic.

The brief period of good Anglo-Egyptian relations which followed the deposition of Farouk in 1952, and the agreement of February 1953, worked fairly well so far as the Sudan was concerned. There was a moment of hesitation in 1955, when it began to look as if internal forces would split the country into north and south, and Britain might need to reconsider her position;[36] but in November of that year it was considered appropriate to withdraw all foreign troops. A transitional constitution, proclaiming the Sudan's status as a 'Sovereign Democratic Republic', was adopted, and at the beginning of 1956 it became completely independent. As with British Somaliland, no effort was made to retain the Sudan within the Commonwealth.

And so, with incredible speed, did all the various British dependent territories north of modern Zambia become independent. The countries concerned differed in almost every imaginable way. In some there was real popular pressure for independence, in others the pressures were slight. Some, perhaps, were 'ready' for self-government; while in others early self-government appeared a likely recipe for civil war.

9
Southern Africa

Most of southern Africa fell within the British Empire in 1945. In all territories, including the Union of South Africa, the population was overwhelmingly black, although white people dominated the area politically and economically. Northern Rhodesia (Zambia), Southern Rhodesia (Zimbabwe) and Nyasaland (Malawi) were under varying measures of British control. The former German colony of South West Africa (Namibia) was a South African Mandated Territory, held under authority of the League of Nations. Three territories bordering the Union – Basutoland (Lesotho), Bechuanaland (Botswana) and Swaziland – ranked as 'High Commission Territories' – British Protectorates within which local rulers preserved a large measure of independence.

Although South Africa was undeniably an independent country, the British Government could not take a detached view of what happened there, for events in the Union were bound to influence developments elsewhere in the British Empire and to some extent in foreign countries as well. The South African General Election of May 1948 would prove of particular importance. The overwhelmingly white electorate dismissed the United Party, headed by Jan Smuts, which had ruled since 1933, and the Nationalist leader, Daniel Malan, was able to form a government. It would be impossible to describe Smuts's policies in racial matters as 'liberal', but those of Malan were a great deal less so and the Nationalists were committed to a policy of apartheid, or separation, of the black and white races.

Racist policies had been endemic in South Africa for a very long time. The Union was established in 1910 by bringing together the

British territories Cape Colony and Natal, and the former Boer republics of Transvaal and the Orange Free State. During the hard negotiations which preceded agreement, the British Government conceded that the franchise in the Union would be the same as that of the component territories. Of the four, only the Cape had made provision for black people to vote. When the colour bar element in the proposed constitution of the Union was challenged in Parliament, Prime Minister Asquith, who very obviously deplored it, explained that 'if this provision of the Bill were to be struck out here, for the time being at any rate, the prospects of Union in South Africa would be wrecked'.[1] No doubt many people envisaged that the South Africans themselves would abandon the colour bar in the foreseeable future; but this was not to be. When they failed to do so, apartheid was a natural development.

People understood 'apartheid' in different ways; but it certainly meant that South Africans were to be divided by law and not just by social custom on the basis of colour; and in practice it meant that the white races nearly always got the better of any arrangement made. In theory, apartheid did not seek to distinguish different white, or different black, races. There were supporters and opponents of the idea among English and Afrikaans speakers alike; but it was particularly popular among Boers, and that point was signalled by Malan's appointment of an exclusively Boer Cabinet. Outside South Africa, apartheid came under more and more criticism; but among the white population of the Union it became increasingly popular. The narrow Nationalist majority of 1948 was increased at the General Elections of 1953 and 1958, eventually becoming an almost 2:1 lead. The Nationalists – first under Malan, then successively under J.G. Strydom and H.F. Verwoerd – pressed further and further in the direction of apartheid.

Few people in Britain approved of the new thrust of South African politics, though it was disliked for very different reasons. Many deplored the attitude the country's new leaders had taken in the recent war. Some were shocked by apartheid; others regretted the overwhelmingly Boer character of the government; many felt apprehensions about the strong anti-Empire and republican proclivities of its leading members. Both the Labour Government of 1945–51 and its Conservative successor appeared uncertain whether to oppose the South African Government vigorously, or whether such opposition would prove counter-productive and merely strengthen the Nationalists' tenure of power.

At first, developments within South Africa – deplorable though they might appear – were not seen to require much response elsewhere. Perhaps there was some feeling that apartheid was a brief storm which would blow over. As time went on, however, apartheid legislation began to bite more and more deeply into South African society. At the same time, countries elsewhere in Africa were moving rapidly towards independence. This exerted a growing influence on people within South Africa, both black and white. Internationally, South Africa became a huge embarrassment to Britain. A great many people did not realise that the country was entirely self-governing, and thought that South African policies were in some way endorsed by Britain. This view received some encouragement when British spokesmen at the United Nations, conscious that South Africa was a member of their own Commonwealth, gave support to the view that her internal actions were not subject to international scrutiny.

In 1959, there were several serious riots in South Africa, linked closely with racial questions and the apartheid policy of the government. Apartheid also took a new twist, for the South African Government introduced legislation designed to create semi-independent 'Bantustans' within the Union, which were designed to become something rather like black protectorates.

Early in 1960, matters developed rapidly. In January, Verwoerd announced his intention to hold a referendum of white voters to decide whether South Africa should become a Republic. Shortly afterwards, Harold Macmillan, in the course of a tour of African countries, made a famous speech to the Cape Town parliament, in the course of which he referred to the 'wind of change' blowing through Africa. The British Prime Minister may or may not have wished to influence South African voters on the referendum question; he certainly hoped to bring them to their senses about the wider matter of relations between black and white people throughout the continent, and the need for South Africa to adapt to changing conditions.

Soon world attention was focused on a major act of violence within the Union. Under the apartheid system, Africans were required to carry passes; a matter which naturally stirred wide resentment. On

21 March 1960, the South African police fired on a large crowd at Sharpeville in the Transvaal, which was protesting against the pass laws: 69 people were killed. On the same day, three more Africans were killed by police at a protest demonstration at Langa, near Cape Town.

In Britain, there was an immediate shock reaction. The Opposition filed a House of Commons motion condemning the killings. That view was widely supported by people of all political persuasions, and put the Government very much on the spot. Prime Minister Macmillan urged the Cabinet 'to observe the convention that one independent member of the Commonwealth should not seek to intervene in the internal affairs of another'. Therefore, in his view, the British Government 'should avoid lending public support to the view that the recent disturbances in South Africa were the inevitable result of the racial policies of the Union Government'.[2] A milder resolution was offered; but ministerial embarrassment was obvious. These matters posed serious difficulties not only in Britain, but also for the Commonwealth as a whole. The Afro-Asian countries were predictably furious at the South African Government, and the meeting of Commonwealth Prime Ministers a few weeks later produced angry recriminations.

Divisions within the Commonwealth ran deep. By early June 1960, Jamaica and Antigua had both imposed bans on trade with South Africa, and there were signs that other West Indian countries would soon do the same. Those countries were at liberty to take their own actions on such matters; but the British Government was more closely involved in another Caribbean country which was still under colonial rule, although this was due to be relinquished in the following year. Ministers in British Guiana, now Guyana, proposed to support a motion in the legislature for a similar ban on trade with South Africa. The colonial Governor sought unsuccessfully to dissuade them. Technically, he was free to reject the motion; but such action would probably be followed by resignation of the ministers and a period of direct rule. If the British Government refused to encourage the Governor to reject the motion, it would be technically in breach of its obligations under the General Agreement on Tariffs and Trade (GATT); if it acted otherwise there was bound to be serious trouble in several parts of the Commonwealth. In the end, the Cabinet decided not to urge rejection, but to risk criticisms from GATT members.[3] As 1960 wore on, the British Government began to take an increasingly principled stand. When the Anglican Bishop of Johannesburg, who had written a book condemning the Sharpeville shootings, was deported from South Africa, Duncan Sandys, Secretary for Commonwealth Relations, publicly condemned the 'most unfortunate impression' this action created.

South Africa itself would soon resolve the stresses which it was generating within the Commonwealth. A referendum on the South African Government's proposal that the country should become a Republic was held on 5 October 1960. By 850,458 votes to 775,878, the white electors decided in favour of the recommendation. Matters were set in motion for the change to take place on 31 May 1961.

When the Commonwealth Prime Ministers met a couple of months before that date, Verwoerd sought to persuade them to permit his country to remain a member of the Commonwealth. Macmillan hoped to secure general agreement to that effect, on the understanding that other Commonwealth countries had the right publicly to oppose South African racial policies. It soon became apparent that several countries would 'conduct a sustained public campaign against the racial policies of the Union government' and might consider leaving the Commonwealth if South Africa remained within it. Macmillan concluded that 'there was a real risk that continued controversy on this issue might have led to the disintegration of the whole association in its present form'.[4] In the end, Verwoerd withdrew his application for continued membership, and South Africa formally left the Commonwealth. In retrospect, one may think that Macmillan would have served the Commonwealth better if he had taken a stronger line from the start.

*

North of the Union lay the two Rhodesias. Immediately before the war of 1939, most people would probably have regarded Southern Rhodesia as the colony next in line for self-government. Ever since the nineteenth century, events there had been deeply influenced by what was happening in South Africa. In the 1890s, the main components of the modern country, Mashonaland and Matabeleland, were brought under control of Cecil Rhodes's 'Chartered Company', and the name Rhodesia came to be used, at first quite unofficially. Enormous slices of land were allocated to favoured white settlers – one man alone receiving 600,000 acres. Even the ultra-imperialist Alfred Milner complained in 1897 that the black people had been 'scandalously used'.[5] The process of land allocation to whites continued for a long time to come. By the 1930s, 28 million acres of Southern Rhodesia, including 'native reserves', were occupied by 1 million black people, while 48 million acres had been acquired by 50,000 whites.

In 1923 the voters of Southern Rhodesia were invited to decide whether their country should receive 'responsible government' or whether it should join South Africa. Some pressure was put on them to take the latter decision – not least by people who feared that South Africa might eventually be dominated by Boers, while a 'British' Rhodesia would be a useful counterpoise within the Union. The voters, all but 60 of whom were white and most of whom were of British extraction, decided otherwise. Southern Rhodesia soon received a considerable measure of autonomy, although the Colonial Office retained some power to control discriminatory legislation.

After 1945, many discussions took place at various levels about future political developments in the area. These discussions frequently linked the future of Southern Rhodesia with that of Northern Rhodesia and Nyasaland. Both places were much more firmly under control of the Colonial Office, which tended to take a paternalistic view of native interests when they conflicted with those of white settlers. Southern Rhodesia was an agricultural producer, with tobacco the major crop, while Northern Rhodesia was an important source of copper. Living standards in both Rhodesias were relatively high. They had similar numbers of black inhabitants, but the Northern territory had only about a quarter as many whites as the South, where they numbered around 200,000. Nyasaland was different. The black population was rather greater than in either of the Rhodesias, but the white population was tiny. Tobacco was grown, but Nyasaland was less important than Southern Rhodesia in world markets.

Many – probably most – of the white residents in the two Rhodesias wished to see the three territories joined and granted Dominion status. It soon emerged, however, that no British Government, Labour or Conservative, would agree to put Africans in the other two countries under a government controlled by settlers, as in Southern Rhodesia. The idea of Federation of the three territories, which had been raised under the 1945–51 Labour Government, was considered actively under the following Conservative administration. The essential argument in favour was that it would be in their economic interest, and that it would create 'a stronger unit of government, which would be better able to resist the infiltration of Afrikaners from the Union of South Africa'.[6] Although the white settlers generally supported Federation, there were early indications that the black population generally opposed it. The government, however, considered that a 'firm lead' from Britain might exert a 'substantial effect on native opinion'. But if there were serious doubts in 1951, at a time when African nationalism was only just beginning to develop as a significant force in other parts of the continent, it is not difficult to see that those doubts would grow as time progressed.

After long negotiations, a sort of solution emerged in 1953. The three colonies were to be joined in the Federation of Rhodesia and Nyasaland – sometimes known as the Central African Federation – within which each would keep its own constitutional structure and relationship with the British Government. The Federation authority would receive powers in certain fields, notably economics, defence, communications and some aspects of education. Thus administration of the Federation was exceptionally complex. Two major British Government Departments were involved – the Colonial Office, which dealt with Nyasaland and Northern Rhodesia, and the Commonwealth Relations Office which dealt with Southern Rhodesia and the Federation itself. Furthermore, the Federation Government was under Colonial Office supervision when dealing with the two northern territories, but not under supervision of either British Department when dealing with Southern Rhodesia.[7] No less complex was the political system under which the Federal Assembly was elected. The Federation electorate was to be the same as that of the individual territories. In Southern Rhodesia, electoral qualifications were related to literacy and income. Theoretically the franchise was not racial, but in practice the overwhelming majority of voters were white. In Northern Rhodesia the vast majority, and in Nyasaland all, of the Africans ranked as British-protected persons, and therefore had no vote.[8]

If the internal workings of the Federation were anomalous, its status within the Commonwealth was no less so. It was not a Dominion and had no immediate prospect of becoming one, yet the legacy of Southern Rhodesia's own 'special relationship' with self-governing Commonwealth countries persisted, and the Federation

Prime Minister was invited to meetings of Commonwealth Prime Ministers – a privilege otherwise granted exclusively to truly independent countries.

In 1956, the Federation began to put pressure on the British Government for developments in the direction of full self-government, like those taking place in the Gold Coast and elsewhere. In the following year, a Franchise Bill was passed by the Federation parliament which – in the view of the British Government – 'represented a substantial advance on the present franchise'. There was some evidence of African dissatisfaction, but the measure was eventually allowed to proceed to Royal Assent.[9] By 1959, however, African opinion in all three territories of the Federation was becoming increasingly disaffected.

Nyasaland, seemingly the least advanced of the three territories, and certainly the weakest economically, was the first epicentre of serious trouble, and many people were disposed to lay the blame – or praise – on Dr Hastings Banda. Banda was born in Nyasaland, but later travelled widely, studying medicine in the United States and Britain. After qualifying, he practised in several parts of the United Kingdom and later in Kenya. While in Britain he had been in contact with Nkrumah and Nyerere, both of whom were at the time obscure private citizens. In 1958, Banda returned to Nyasaland, where he concentrated his attention on political matters.

Early in March 1959, there was sufficient turbulence in Nyasaland to induce the government to proclaim a State of Emergency, and Banda was arrested. By the end of the month, 52 people had been killed by the security forces, and a further 953 were detained. There was an outcry in Britain, and the Government set up a Commission, under Mr Justice Devlin, to investigate the matter. The Devlin Commission supported the need for emergency powers in Nyasaland, but criticised the development of a 'police state', deplored 'unnecessary arrests' and 'illegal force' and – perhaps most disturbing of all to the British Government and the Federation authorities – noted the 'deep rooted and almost universal opposition to Federation' among the Africans in Nyasaland.

African hostility towards the Federation continued to grow, now that territories with black populations were advancing rapidly towards independence elsewhere in Africa. A State of Emergency was proclaimed in February for Southern Rhodesia. African National

Congresses (ANCs) were banned in the territory, and many arrests were made. Matters had quietened down sufficiently for the Emergency to be ended in May, but the Southern Rhodesian Prime Minister, Sir Edgar Whitehead, acknowledged the need to remove 'real grievances' of the African people and 'unnecessary discrimination', which had played a part in causing the disturbances.

The British Cabinet was also plainly unhappy with the view of the situation in Nyasaland which they were receiving from the Federation authorities. Colonial Secretary Iain Macleod persuaded his colleagues to put pressure on the Federation authorities to support the release of Dr Banda and to enter serious consultations about the future of the territory. To these suggestions both Whitehead and the Federal Prime Minister Sir Roy Welensky reacted in an 'extremely critical' manner.[10]

By the middle of February Macmillan was warning his Cabinet colleagues that the Federation itself was unlikely to secure sufficient African confidence to survive unless some constitutional advance was made in Nyasaland.[11] He also recognised the compensating risk 'that Southern Rhodesia might secede from the Federation, or that the Federal government might make a unilateral declaration of independence'. This appears to be the first reference in Cabinet minutes to that sinister expression. After some further delay, the British Government ordered the release of Banda.

Meanwhile, the British Government had set up a Royal Commission under Viscount Monckton, who had served in Eden's Cabinet, to investigate the workings of the Federation. When the Monckton Commission reported in October 1960, it upheld many of the Africans' grievances. Although it considered that the Federation should be retained, yet it acknowledged that African hostility would continue unless there were 'drastic and fundamental changes both in the structure of the association itself and in the racial policies of Southern Rhodesia'. What particularly shocked Welensky was the Commission's recommendation that the British Government should declare its intention to permit territories to secede from the Federation. There was intense argument as to whether the Commission was exceeding its terms of reference by making such a proposal. By this date, indeed, the Federation authorities were fighting a war on two fronts: against disaffected black activists, and against some white Southern Rhodesians who complained that the Federation was moving too rapidly in the Africans' direction. The Monckton Commission also recommended that there should be an African majority on the Legislative Council of Northern Rhodesia.[12]

A Constitutional Conference to consider the country's future was held early in 1961. The talks were inconclusive, but by February 1962 even Welensky came to realise that 'any constitution for Northern Rhodesia would be likely to produce an anti-Federal majority', while 'there was already a large anti-Federal majority in Nyasaland'. Thus two of the three territories already possessed the will, and were likely soon to possess the power, to leave the Federation. At this point, the Cabinet made a belated effort to cut through the administration absurdities affecting British relations with the Federation, and gave special responsibility to R.A. Butler, probably the second most influential man in the government.

Several months more of discussions followed. At last, late in October 1962, Butler brought the Cabinet to acknowledge that Nyasaland at any rate must be allowed to withdraw, even though 'it would inevitably lead in time to the dissolution of the Federation as such'.[13] There were further anguished negotiations with the Federation authorities, but at last, on 19 December, the British Government stated that view publicly. Welensky's reaction was explosive: 'the British Government have ratted on us'; the British statement was 'an act of treachery'.

While the debate over Nyasaland's right to secede from the Federation was moving towards the inevitable decision, parallel discussions over plans for self-government there were proceeding apace. In November 1962, a Constitutional Conference was held in London, and 'complete agreement' was recorded. The new Constitution would be linked with a Bill of Rights, protecting the rights of the European minority. At the beginning of February 1963, internal self-government took effect and Banda became Prime Minister. The Federal authorities felt considerable alarm about the country's future prospects. J.M. Greenfield, Federal Minister of Law, observed 'the woeful shortage of lawyers in Nyasaland', noting that 'the only qualified African has become the Minister of Justice'. He feared that 'the Bill of Rights would become a mockery'.[14] One may guess that there were similar deficiencies in qualified administrators of other kinds. Plans were nevertheless set in motion for Nyasaland to become completely independent in July 1964, under the new name Malawi.

The status of Malawi had been planned some time before, and agreement reached between Banda and the Governor. The country would maintain allegiance to the Crown for a short period. This would allow the 'stabilising influence of the Governor' to be retained, while the future Constitution could be worked out without undue haste.[15] This plan was roughly followed, and Malawi became a Republic within the Commonwealth in 1966.

Northern Rhodesia was moving rapidly in the same direction. Elections were held at the end of October 1962 and resulted in voting on largely racial lines. After some delay, a coalition was formed between the African parties – Kenneth Kaunda's United National Independence Party (UNIP) and Harry Nkumbula's African National Congress – both of which were opposed to the Federation. In March 1963, the British Government acknowledged the right of any territory, and not just Nyasaland, to secede. Soon the Southern Rhodesian Government, once the main bastion of the Federation, also began to mount pressure for independence.

'Independence' for Southern Rhodesia meant a very different thing from independence for Northern Rhodesia or Nyasaland, for under existing constitutional arrangements the colony was largely controlled by the white settler minority. In September 1962, long before hope for the Federation had been abandoned, the principal African political organisation, Zimbabwe African People's Union (ZAPU) was banned, and most Africans boycotted the elections which were held in the territory in the following December. Two main parties entered the lists. The United Federal Party, which included African as well as European members, wished to continue the Federation. It was opposed to racially discriminatory practices and sought to repeal the Land Apportionment Acts, which allocated specific areas within the territory to Europeans, and others to Africans.[16] The Rhodesia Front, headed by Winston Field, pointedly deplored 'forced integration' of the races. The upshot of the election was a rather narrow win for the Rhodesia Front. Field formed a government which was anxious to maintain the domestic status quo, and sought independence for Southern Rhodesia as soon as possible.

By May 1963, it became apparent to the British Government that 'if we granted independence to Southern Rhodesia without stipulating that the present constitution should be ordered on more liberal lines, the other members of the Commonwealth would not be prepared to accept her as a fellow-member'.[17] Furthermore, this attitude was not confined to the Afrasians, who 'might well decide to leave the Commonwealth altogether'; it was also likely to be adopted by 'the older members of the Commonwealth'. Yet, the Cabinet decided, it was 'very unlikely' that Southern Rhodesia would be prepared to accept the constitutional changes which were necessary.

The Federation authorities at last accepted the inevitability of breakdown. At the turn of June and July 1963, a conference was held at Victoria Falls to prepare dissolution of the Federation. Agreement was reached that it should end on 31 December 1963. Division of the Federation's assets and liabilities was also agreed.

Early in 1964, a new constitution took effect in Northern Rhodesia. Shortly afterwards, elections resulted in a large overall majority for UNIP, and Kaunda formed a government. Arrangements went ahead for the establishment of a full independent state, under the name Zambia, which came into existence in October. Zambia elected to remain a member of the Commonwealth; but, unlike most former African dependencies, became a Republic immediately on attaining independence.

Many important changes took place in the character of Southern Rhodesia and its politics during 1964. After Northern Rhodesia became independent, the name of the country was changed to Rhodesia. The position of Winston Field became increasingly difficult. A strong advocate of Rhodesian independence, he was much less keen on the idea of a 'unilateral declaration of independence' (UDI) which was becoming increasingly popular among the less thoughtful members of the Rhodesian Front. In April, the Front's 'caucus' resolved to dismiss him.[18] Perhaps Field could have fought back successfully; but his health was not good and he resigned the premiership. The successor was Ian Smith.

For much of the year, there were many discussions about the future between the Governments of Britain and Rhodesia. The new Rhodesian Prime Minister, like his predecessor, evidently hoped that agreement over independence could be reached with the British Government, but Smith contemplated UDI as a last resort. On the suggestion of Britain, Canada, Australia and New Zealand all put what pressure they could on Rhodesia to desist from UDI.[19]

Meanwhile, organs of the United Nations urged Britain not to grant independence to Rhodesia until representative institutions had been established.

Smith visited London in September for discussions with the British Government. He claimed that independence had the support of most Rhodesians, African as well as European, and proposed to establish the truth of that assertion by 'traditional tribal consultation'. This meant summoning an *indaba,* or conference of chiefs and other leaders, which duly decided in favour of independence. That result was less impressive than appeared to be the case. The chiefs were mostly elderly and were paid by the government. They might be regarded as government officials for practical purposes.

In October 1964, a General Election in Britain produced a small Labour majority and a new government was formed, headed by Harold Wilson. Its attitude to the Rhodesian question was more or less the same as that of its predecessor. Almost immediately, the Prime Minister declared that UDI would constitute 'rebellion'. The Smith Government in Rhodesia had already planned a referendum on the independence issue, to be held early in November; but it also announced that a positive vote would not constitute a mandate for UDI. The referendum went overwhelmingly in favour of independence, though a large majority of Africans abstained from voting. Early in 1965, another approach was tried. The funeral of Sir Winston Churchill in January was the occasion for many Commonwealth representatives, including Smith, to visit London. A meeting with Wilson was contrived, but it proved a dismal failure.[20]

Unpropitious as the political omens were, the principal personalities, British and Rhodesian alike, seemed anxious to avoid the final break which UDI would represent, and for most of 1965 discussions continued at various levels. In May, new elections gave the Rhodesia Front an overwhelming majority. This included every one of the predominantly white 'A' roll seats. But there were also powerful forces at work in a very different direction. When a new meeting of Commonwealth Prime Ministers was held in June 1965, the African representatives proposed that Britain should suspend the Rhodesian constitution and impose direct rule if the administration refused to accept drastic constitutional changes. Yet there was no realistic chance of compelling Rhodesia to accept direct rule, save by force – which was really out of the question. There was again a serious threat that the Rhodesian question would disrupt the Commonwealth.

Further attempts were made to secure a settlement which would avert UDI. Wilson flew to Rhodesia in October and met leaders of all the significant opinion groups. He appeared to reach agreement with Smith on the idea of appointing a Royal Commission to ascertain whether the people of Rhodesia as a whole accepted the idea of independence on the basis of the country's 1961 constitution. But arguments soon developed over what would be the Commission's terms of reference, and by early November something near deadlock had developed.

There may well have been a good deal of brinkmanship on both sides. On 9 November, the British Cabinet[21] received an apparently reliable report to the effect that the Rhodesian Cabinet was divided – Smith still favouring a Royal Commission, but with strong pressure developing in favour of immediate UDI. Smith sought a private assurance that if a Royal Commission reported that the people of Rhodesia as a whole favoured independence, the British Government would recommend Parliament to accept it. But would the Rhodesians be prepared to make a similar gesture if the report went against their wishes?[22] A few days earlier, a compromise agreement on such lines might perhaps have averted UDI, but it was too late. The Prime Minister communicated the tentative suggestion to Smith by telephone, but received the bleak reply 'that the positions of the two governments were irreconcilable'.[23] In the morning of 11 November – at the very moment when the British Cabinet was discussing the issue – UDI was announced.

Both sides reacted with great speed. The Governor of Rhodesia formally dismissed Smith and his administration. Predictably, the dismissal was ignored. A new 'constitution' was proclaimed by the Rhodesian rebels, with provision for an 'Officer administering the Government' to perform the functions of the Governor. On the same day, the British banned importation of Rhodesian tobacco and sugar and enforced restrictions on exchange. Further economic measures, which included freezing whatever Rhodesian foreign reserves could be reached, and also an oil embargo, soon followed. No foreign government seemed disposed formally to recognise the rebel Rhodesian regime, but South Africa continued normal relations. So also did Portugal, whose colony Mozambique gave Rhodesia access to the sea.

*

In 1945, there were four territories adjoining South Africa to which the Union Government lay special claim. Although the three 'High Commission Territories' had not been incorporated in South Africa in 1910, it was contemplated (though never promised) that they might later be joined to the new Union. At the end of the Second World War, they had a combined population of around a million, and all of them sent many workers into the Union.

At the end of the war, South West Africa (Namibia) was still a League of Nations Mandate, held by the South African Government. As in many parts of Africa, the indigenous peoples had long-established grounds of grievance. The pre-1914 German Government had confiscated great areas of 'native' land. Under the Mandate, the South African Government proceeded to establish white settlers. Legislation ostensibly designed to control 'vagrancy' was introduced, whose real purpose was to compel 'natives' to work for white farmers.[24] In 1925, an Assembly with limited legislative powers had been set up. Although the vast majority of the population was black, the electorate was exclusively white.

When the League of Nations was formally dissolved in 1946, most League Mandates soon became Trust Territories held by the Mandatory Power with the authority of the United Nations. South Africa – still under the Smuts régime – unsuccessfully sought permission to annex South West Africa. The Nationalist Government which took power in 1948 favoured a rather different approach towards the same objective. In 1949, the Union Parliament passed an Act giving six seats in the House of Assembly and four in the Senate to representatives of South West Africa.

The line between South West Africa's condition and the status of a 'fifth Province' of the Union was becoming a fine one indeed. Apartheid laws were applied to South West Africa, and further lands belonging to the indigenous peoples were appropriated. These measures were condemned by the United Nations, and in 1971 the International Court of Justice ruled that the effective annexation of the country by South Africa was unlawful. Little could be done, however, to make such protests effective until the apartheid régime in South Africa began to disintegrate in 1989, and South West Africa, renamed Namibia, emerged as an independent Republic, which became part of the Commonwealth.

The fate of the three 'High Commission Territories' was different. South Africa never sought to annex them unlawfully, although she certainly hoped eventually to do so legally, and in the meantime attempted to influence British policy. The most famous example of this influence, which attracted much world attention at the time, concerned the 100,000 or so Bamangwato, who were one of the principal tribes in Bechuanaland.[25] British administration was con-ducted through tribal institutions. The designate chief was Seretse Khama, who had succeeded his father while a boy, and had spent most of his manhood as a student abroad, while his uncle Tshekedi Khama acted as regent. A British Government memorandum reported that Tshekedi ruled 'efficiently but rigorously and perhaps sometimes harshly'.[26]

In 1948, Seretse married a white woman, despite efforts of both British and Bamangwato officials to dissuade him. Three tribal meet-ings were held to discuss the matter, and the final one produced a large majority in Seretse's favour. The British Government did not wish to upset the Governments of South Africa and Southern Rhodesia (which also bordered Bechuanaland), and so the High Commissioner inaugurated a judicial inquiry, which decided that Seretse was not a suitable person to be chief. The Labour Government in Britain agreed with these findings, but decided that it would be impolitic to publish the report. In March 1950, however, it announced that recognition of Seretse would be withheld for not less than five years.[27] As Tshekedi's regency had ended, the British District Commissioner exercised the functions of the Bamangwato authority. Tshekedi and Seretse were both excluded from the territory.

Shortly after the Conservatives returned to power in 1951, the new Government decided[28] that Seretse should be excluded perma-nently; that Tshekedi might be allowed to return later as a private citizen; while a third member of the Khama family, Rasebolai, should be built up as prospective chief. An unsuccessful attempt was made to mollify Seretse by offer of a government job in Jamaica.

Eventually, Seretse renounced all claim on the chieftainship and was allowed to return to his country.

Seretse Khama soon reappeared in public life in a new capacity. In 1961 he became a member of the Executive Council of the Protectorate. In the following year, he founded the Democratic Party, which won 28 out of 31 seats when the first elections were held in 1965. Seretse Khama thereupon become Prime Minister. It was soon agreed that the country should become a Republic within the Commonwealth, under the new name Botswana, in September 1966. Seretse Khama was appointed the first President. A curious sidelight on Commonwealth practices was provided by the decision to award Seretse a British knighthood shortly before he became Head of State of an independent sovereign Republic.

The other High Commission Territories followed rather similar courses of constitutional development to Botswana. Political parties appeared in the late 1950s and early 1960s, while the British authorities responded willingly to local demands for independence. In some respects, however, there were significant differences. In Basutoland, events followed a rather turbulent course. The first elections, held in 1965, were attended by a threat of violence, which was averted only by strict security measures. The moderate National Party won by a narrow margin, with the Congress Party, believed to have communist links, not far behind. The British nevertheless promised full independence in the following year. So Basutoland, now renamed Lesotho, became independent in October 1966, less than a week after Botswana. The country became a monarchy within the Commonwealth.

Swaziland, most prosperous of the three High Commission Territories, was also the last to achieve independence. In 1966, the British Government promised self-government in the following year, and full independence before the end of 1969. In the 1967 elections, the Imbokodvo Party won every seat, and the British were soon persuaded to advance the date of independence to September 1968. Like Lesotho, Swaziland chose to become a monarchy within the Commonwealth. With the independence of Swaziland, British imperial power in Africa came to an end.

10
Smaller Colonies

While Britain was withdrawing from her great possessions in Asia and was preparing to withdraw from Africa, the future of many of her remaining colonies was called into question.

Cyprus had escaped enemy occupation in 1939–45, and when the war ended the Greek Government was far too anxious to secure British military and economic assistance to bother about asserting claims to this mainly Greek island. Meanwhile, the British Government found Cyprus a convenient dumping-ground for illegal Jewish immigrants who were seeking entry to Palestine. A new constitution was offered in 1948, but the leading Cypriots rejected it. Early in 1950, a plebiscite organised by the Greek religious authorities showed overwhelming support for *enosis*, or union with Greece.

Not long after this, a new Archbishop of Cyprus, Makarios III, was installed. The name means 'blessed', but he was usually known to British soldiers as 'Black Mac', or 'MacHarris'. As in other Eastern Mediterranean lands, Greek religious leaders had political functions as well, which had been recognised in Ottoman times and long before. The alternative title of the Archbishop was ethnarch – 'leader of the nation'. Makarios sought to revive interest in the idea of *enosis* among both Greek and British authorities. Thus the 'national' struggle, which in most colonial countries aimed at independence, in Cyprus sought transfer from British rule to rule by another country. Down to 1954, there was 'considerable apathy among the people of Cyprus',[1] but in that year the Greek Government began to press its claims to the island seriously, and attitudes changed swiftly. Predictably, the British Chiefs of Staff advised the

Government that it was 'essential for strategic reasons that we should retain full sovereignty'.[2]

At the end of 1954, there were riots in Cyprus. In March of the following year, just a few days before Churchill left office, a protracted campaign of violence began. In November 1955, a 'State of Emergency' was proclaimed. The British authorities were disposed to put much of the blame for the disturbances on Makarios, and for a time he, and a number of other ecclesiastics, were deported to the Seychelles. For several years, violence continued in fits and starts. The Turkish minority was generally quiet. But whatever the British, Greek and Turkish Governments, and the indigenous Cypriot peoples, might think of each other, most of them were a good deal more worried still about the threat from Russia. NATO meetings at the end of 1958 provided a useful occasion for contacts between the three governments, and early in 1959 a new plan emerged, which proved acceptable to the negotiators.[3]

Cyprus was to become a Republic, with a Greek President and a Turkish Vice-President. The Council of Ministers, the House of Representatives, the civil service, the security forces and the army were all to include Greeks and Turks in the fixed proportions. There would be no partition, and no union with any other state. A Treaty guaranteeing the independence, territorial integrity and constitution of the island was to be concluded between the new Republic, Turkey, Greece and the United Kingdom. These arrangements were based on the idea that power in the island could be shared by hitherto hostile indigenous peoples, rather than territory being divided between them. Britain was authorised to retain sovereignty over two small base areas.

Prisoners were released, the Emergency was ended and, in December 1959, Makarios was appointed President-elect. In August 1960, the new Republic was formally inaugurated. Almost immediately, troubles began again; but from Britain's point of view both the advantages and the burdens of imperial responsibility had been relinquished. In 1961 – with agreement from both Greeks and Turks on the island – the Republic joined the Commonwealth.[4]

Another important Mediterranean base also underwent major changes. Malta came under British control early in the nineteenth century. The dockyard eventually became pivotal to the whole economy. During the Second World War, the people suffered so badly from enemy bombardment, and behaved so bravely, that the George Cross was awarded in recognition. In 1945, Malta had a population in excess of 300,000 crammed into a largely infertile area considerably smaller than the Isle of Wight. Unlike Cyprus, Malta had no strong ethnic affinities with other countries and nobody coveted it; but it soon ran into economic difficulties. The massive British defence spending of the past was being scaled down and in the early 1950s both the Maltese and the British began to give serious consideration to the future.

Two very different lines of possible constitutional development came under discussion. Malta might become independent; or it might be integrated more or less completely into the United Kingdom. The Nationalist Party, headed by Dr Borg Oliver, inclined to the former solution, the Maltese Labour Party, headed by Dom Mintoff, to the latter.

In 1955, the Labour Party took office in Malta. A few months later, a Conference was convened in London, attended by representatives of a wide range of British and Maltese opinion. The upshot was a Report supported by nearly all participants, which made various proposals relating to Malta's future. On the constitutional question, it decided that a solution on what were sometimes called 'Ulster' lines was practicable and reasonable. Malta would retain its own parliament for domestic affairs, but would also send MPs to Westminster. It was generally agreed, however, that it would be necessary to consult the Maltese people before any action was taken.

A plebiscite was held in February 1956, at which around 74 per cent voted in favour of integration. On closer inspection, however, results were much less convincing. The very influential Archbishop of Malta, who feared erosion of the Catholic Church's privileged position, had urged abstention, and so had the Nationalists. This advice was evidently widely followed. The poll was therefore low, and the vote in favour represented only 45 per cent of the total electorate. The British Government accordingly decided to suspend implementation of the constitutional proposals until Maltese opinion had been tested again, this time through a General Election.

There followed discussions in London on financial implications of integration. As talks proceeded, the British became less eager to assume the various responsibilities which integration seemed to imply. The upshot was that Mintoff, who had been the principal advocate of integration, swung very much the other way and began to campaign for complete independence. In April 1958 his Government resigned. No alternative administration seemed available, and the Governor assumed control. There were violent demonstrations and a State of Emergency was proclaimed. Over several years, various unsuccessful attempts were made to resolve the deadlock.

Early in 1962, there were elections in Malta. No party won an overall majority, but the Nationalists were the largest single group and Oliver was able to form a government, which soon requested independence within the Commonwealth. After much further discussion, the Nationalists prepared a new constitution, on which a referendum was held in May 1964. The results were as inconclusive as those of the plebiscite held eight years earlier. After this, the British and Maltese Governments negotiated directly on future constitutional, financial and defence arrangements. Agreement was eventually reached to the effect that Malta should become fully independent. Britain would lubricate the deal by grants and loans totalling £50 million, spread over the ensuing ten years. On this basis, independence was proclaimed in September 1964. For ten years the Queen remained Head of State, but in 1974 Malta became a Republic within the Commonwealth.

The importance of this long and complex struggle lies not just in the result eventually achieved for Malta, but also in its implications elsewhere. There were many British dependent territories which, like Malta, were considerably smaller than most sovereign states. If Malta had been incorporated in the United Kingdom – an upshot which had seemed very likely in the mid-1950s – there was a real prospect that it might be emulated in other places, which would have had important long-term consequences both for those places and for Britain.

*

With the Mediterranean colonies, as with the much greater possessions in Asia and Africa, Britain's main problem had been to deal with indigenous peoples. Further on the traditional route to the East, in Aden, the difficulties were much more complex, for they involved aspects of the 'Cold War', the economics of Middle Eastern oil and the rising force of Arab nationalism. Arab nationalism was a very different proposition from African nationalism. African nationalists sought only to establish independent African states in places currently held by Europeans. Some of the Arab nationalists dreamed of creating a great empire of Arabic-speaking peoples which would extend from the Mahgreb to Iraq. Such an empire, if it came into existence, would be a major force in world politics, comparable with the United States or the Soviet Union.

Aden had been acquired by Britain as far back as 1838. In the 1950s, the Colony of Aden consisted of little more than Aden town and the refinery port of Little Aden nearby, with a total population of around 85,000, most of whom were immigrants from Yemen. The Colony was linked with a much larger Protectorate, extending along much of the southern shore of the Arabian peninsula. In the view of the Governor, the petty states within the Protectorate were mostly 'primitive tribal autocracies riven by rivalries, feuds and jealousies'.[5]

The Suez débâcle and its aftermath gave Aden a much greater importance for general British policy. Nasser acquired a massive prestige throughout the Arab world and his desire to extend Egyptian influence as widely as possible was never in doubt. At the same time, the Soviet Union was adopting an increasingly active role in Middle Eastern affairs. As an 'imperialist' possession with an Arab population, Aden was a natural target for criticism from both angles. Britain's continuing interest in Aden was essentially strategic: as a base to secure access to Middle Eastern oil, and as a link in communications with places further east, particularly Singapore.[6]

In the course of 1958, the Governor of Aden, the Colonial Office and eventually the British Government came to accept the view that it would be impossible to retain Aden as a colony indefinitely; but that it was realistic to envisage the development of a 'friendly state' from the western part of the Protectorate, perhaps including the Colony as well. Such a state might eventually become part of the Commonwealth.[7]

A new Constitution was devised for the Colony. This took effect at the beginning of 1959 and provided for some places on the Legislative Council to be filled by elections. Unfortunately, no political parties, in the ordinary sense of the term, had emerged; while the powerful Aden TUC boycotted the elections. Thus the moral authority of the Aden legislature which resulted was not very great. About the same time, however, developments in the Protectorate seemed more encouraging to the British Government, and it was able to coax into existence an entity which later became known as the Federation of South Arabia. The rulers in the Federation soon became attracted to the idea of closer union with each other and there was also much discussion about forging links between the Federation and Aden Colony. The Aden legislature approved, although there was strong reason for thinking that the idea was unpopular among the people of the Colony.[8] In Britain, the proposal was contested in Parliament by both opposition parties, but nevertheless took effect early in 1963.

More trouble was already brewing. In 1962, there was a revolution in the independent state of the Yemen, immediately to the north of the Federation, and Egyptian influence was widely seen.

In October 1964, a Labour Government took office in Britain. By this time, there was no prospect of holding the line for much longer and the best that Britain could hope for was a dignified withdrawal, leaving a friendly and peaceful state behind. Towards the end of the year, the new Colonial Secretary, Anthony Greenwood, told his Cabinet colleagues[9] that 'our policy was directed towards the establishment of a fully independent Arab state by 1968 at the latest'. But violence broke out with increasing severity in Colony and Federation alike, while international pressure was exerted through the United Nations for Britain to leave Aden. Early in 1966, it was announced that she would do so in 1968, when the Federation of South Arabia was to become independent. Before that date, however, the whole character of the Federation changed beyond recognition. In the course of August and September 1967, one of the populist groups captured control of all sixteen sultanates in the Federation.

In the course of November 1967, several important events occurred almost simultaneously. Egyptian troops were withdrawn from the Yemen; British troops were pulled out of both Aden Colony and the Federation. Before the end of the month, a new independent state, known as the People's Republic of South Yemen, had been set up on the ruins of the erstwhile Colony and Protectorate, while Britain was committed to paying a substantial sum which would help restore the trade of the port and the output of the refinery.

*

In southern Arabia, as in Central Africa, a Federation had been set up under British auspices during the 1950s with the avowed object of strengthening weak units through a measure of political union. Both Federations collapsed ignominiously within a decade. There are some parallels with events in the Caribbean area about the same time.

Britain had a number of colonial possessions in the region. The Lesser Antilles form a chain of islands fringing the Atlantic, making an arc about 600 miles long, extending from the Virgin Islands and Anguilla in the north to Trinidad in the south. Most of the islands were British, but Guadeloupe and Martinique, around the middle of the chain, were French, and some of the Virgin Islands belonged to the United States. Hundreds of miles to the west lay Jamaica, which was linked politically with the Cayman islands, and the Turks & Caicos islands. On the mainland of Central America was British Honduras (Belize). A couple of hundred miles from Trinidad, along the coast of South America, lay British Guiana (Guyana). The Bahamas, lying north of Cuba, were treated separately from the other islands throughout all discussions. Of all the British West Indies, by far the most populous was Jamaica, where more than half of the three million inhabitants of the islands lived. Trinidad and the associated island of Tobago had about 750,000 inhabitants, and Barbados rather fewer than 250,000. None of the other islands had as many as 100,000.

The inhabitants of the islands were of mixed racial origin, although the original Caribs were nearly extinct. Descendants of slaves imported from Africa during the eighteenth century for the sugar plantations formed the principal element in the population, but many people were of partly European descent. The racial admixture had become so complete over time that ethnic problems like those which vexed many parts of the British Empire were not acute.

The British West Indian colonies had a record of much turbulence in earlier times, particularly in the period of slavery and its immediate aftermath, but in the twentieth century they had been, on the whole, more peaceful, and some of them had been developing gradually in the direction of internal self-government. There was serious turmoil in some of the islands in the inter-war period, but this was related more to economic and social grievances than to nationalism, and a Royal Commission reported at the end of 1939, recommending sweeping changes. During the war, there were also significant political developments. Thus, Jamaica received a relatively liberal constitution in 1944.

The idea that some, or all, of the West Indies should be joined politically was an old one. The Leeward Islands had been linked together for certain purposes from the late nineteenth century, and that particular unit was not dissolved until 1956. In 1953, however, plans began to be made for a Federation of the British West Indies, which was to include the islands, but (at least at the beginning) not the two mainland territories. Establishment of the Federation took place in a rather leisurely manner. The local legislatures approved and a federal constitution was drafted. After much discussion, it was agreed that the federal capital should be on Trinidad.

The first Federal elections were held in March 1958, with universal adult franchise. Two large parties took the field. Both were organised on a Federal basis, but had their roots in existing Government and opposition parties on the individual islands. The Federal Labour Party won a rather small overall majority, and Sir Grantley Adams of Barbados became Prime Minister.

Initial signs for the Federation's prospects were not encouraging.[10] No substantial federal issues were raised in the election. The poll was light; even in politically conscious Jamaica only 40 per cent of the electorate bothered to vote. Adams was the only major political figure to offer himself for election; the others evidently considered the affairs of their own islands more important. The opposition party, confusingly known as the Democratic Labour Party, won a substantial majority of the seats from Jamaica and Trinidad; the main strength of the Federal Labour Party lay in Barbados and the smaller islands.

Plans were nevertheless made for the West Indies Federation to advance to independence in May 1962, in the reasonable hope that it would soon become a full member of the Commonwealth. In September 1961, however, these plans were thrown completely awry by a referendum in Jamaica to consider whether the island should leave the Federation. On a 60 per cent poll, the islanders voted by 251,935 to 216,400 to secede. The Jamaican Prime Minister Norman Manley accepted the verdict. Thus Jamaica's withdrawal became certain.

For a time there seemed to be a possibility that the Federation would continue, with leadership from Trinidad, whose large population and important resources of oil and asphalt gave it a clear claim for primacy now that Jamaica had withdrawn. Soon, however, the Trinidadians decided that the burden of the other islands would be too great to bear. The Federation collapsed, and in February 1962 preparations were made to dissolve it.[11] Plans also went ahead for Jamaica, and for Trinidad & Tobago, to become independent members of the Commonwealth. These took effect later in 1962.

When Jamaica and Trinidad withdrew from the Federation, there still seemed to be an outside chance of salvaging something from the wreck. In February 1965, a Regional Council of smaller West Indian islands drew up a plan for a new Federation which would centre on Barbados. That idea was effectively killed when a conference of the ruling party on the island defeated a pro-Federal resolution, endorsing instead a demand for independence. In 1966, independence was accordingly granted to Barbados.

In the course of 1966, plans went ahead for most of the remaining West Indies to become 'Associate States of the United Kingdom', with complete control of their internal affairs, but with the United Kingdom retaining responsibility for defence and external relations. This was probably never visualised as much more than a stop-gap. In the course of the 1970s and early 1980s, the more populous West Indian islands, and the Bahamas as well, became independent states within the Commonwealth. Unlike the former African colonies, most of the West Indian islands wished the Queen to remain Head of State, although Trinidad became a Republic within the Commonwealth in 1974.

When the West Indies Federation was established in 1958, provisions were made for the possible accession of British Guiana and British Honduras at a later date. Long before the Federation collapsed, however, it became evident that the two mainland colonies were likely to develop in a different way from the islands. There was a great population mix in British Guiana. The country's 640,000 inhabitants[12] were made up of roughly 320,000 'East Indians', 200,000 Africans, 30,000 Amerindians, 76,000 people of mixed origin, and 13,000 others – including Portuguese, Chinese and British. As many of the immigrants had arrived comparatively recently, there had been less integration, and there were racial overtones to the colony's politics.

In 1953, a new constitution took effect in British Guiana. When elections were held in April, the only organised political movement was Dr Cheddi Jagan's People's Progressive Party, which captured three-quarters of the seats. Five months later, the Colonial Secretary complained that the PPP had 'taken every opportunity to undermine the constitution and to further the communist cause'.[13] Perhaps the word 'communist' was being used loosely; but in any event the constitution of British Guiana was suspended at the end of 1953, and for three years interim arrangements were followed. Late in 1956, a new constitution was granted, with a substantially less democratic structure than before. Elections of the following year again gave a large majority to the PPP, and Jagan again became Chief Minister. During the next few years, several further attempts were made to achieve agreement between the British Government and the ministers in British Guiana about the country's constitutional future.

In 1957, a major split in the PPP resulted in the formation of a new political party, the People's National Congress, under the leadership of Forbes Burnham. Not least of the problems thereafter was the extent to which 'the political situation in British Guiana reflected the growing tensions between the Indian and African elements of the population':[14] the former group supporting the PPP, the latter the PNC.

For several years, matters drifted on. Civil order began gradually to break down. By early July 1963, Colonial Secretary Sandys was reporting a bleak situation to the Cabinet. A General Strike with strong political overtones was in its tenth week; racial riots were increasing and additional British troops were required to maintain order. With visible frustration, he complained that 'In normal circumstances the colony would by now have attained independence; but Dr Jagan's government was not only Communist in its sympathies but also incapable of maintaining order unaided'.[15]

This was the nadir. Soon the strike ended, and a few months later it was possible to hold a constitutional conference in London to plan the colony's future. Representatives of the British Guiana political parties failed to agree on several major issues, but – perhaps surprisingly – declared themselves willing to abide by British arbitration. The upshot was that new elections were planned for the following year, to be held with proportional representation and supervised by an independent commission.

Violence still flared up from time to time, but by December 1964 matters had settled down sufficiently for elections to be held. The PPP secured more votes and more seats than any other party, but fell substantially short of an overall majority. After some delay, the PNC leader Forbes Burnham was able to form a government with support from a small third party. Soon plans were prepared for the colony to advance towards independence, although the colonial government requested Britain to keep troops there for long enough to enable a local security force to be trained. In May 1965, British Guiana became an independent member of the Commonwealth, under the name Guyana.

At one point in 1953, it had seemed that the much smaller mainland colony British Honduras would suffer from problems comparable with those of British Guiana.[16] The first political party to emerge, the People's United Party, was declared to be 'violently anti-British', and was believed to receive financial support from Guatemala, which had long laid claim to the colony. The worst apprehensions were not realised. Elections in 1957, and further elections in the following year, left the PUP firmly in control of the Legislative Council; but in January 1959 the British Government was relieved to learn that a resolution had been passed affirming loyalty to the Queen and rejecting Guatemalan claims. Thereafter, events moved relatively smoothly. Internal self-government took effect at the beginning of 1964, although full independence within the Commonwealth, under the new name Belize, was not achieved until 1981.

*

Although the idea of federating small colonies or protectorates proved a failure in the West Indies, as it had also done in Central Africa and southern Arabia, it was much more successful in South-East Asia. The Malayan 'Emergency' which began in 1948 did not seriously impede constitutional reconstruction. The United Malays National Organisation which had originally been formed in 1946 broadened into what became known as the Alliance Party, under the leadership of Tunku Abdul Rahman, half-brother of the Sultan of Kedah. Soon the Alliance was pressing for elections to the Legislative Council, and it was agreed that 52 out of 98 members should be elected. When the first elections were held in July 1955, all but one of the elective seats were taken by the Alliance Party, and the Tunku became Chief Minister. Soon afterwards, an amnesty was offered to the rebels in the guerilla conflict, but was not accepted. Then the Chief Minister took an initiative of his own and went into the jungle to meet their leaders. This also came to nothing. The Malayan Government was much more successful in its dealings with Britain. In February 1956, a delegation of ministers and representatives of the rulers visited London, and the Colonial Secretary was able to report to the Cabinet that 'all the issues before the Conference had been settled amicably'.[17] Independence was granted to Malaya in August 1957. The States retained the large measure of autonomy which they had received under the 1948 federal constitution. Malaya became a constitutional monarchy with its own Head of State, who was elected every five years, while it recognised the Queen as Head of the Commonwealth.

The Federation of Malaya later contrived to incorporate three places which were still British colonies in 1957. In Singapore, the 1948 Emergency involved less violence than in Malaya, but communists were able to establish considerable influence, particularly in trade unions and schools. During the 1950s, when colonies elsewhere were advancing rapidly towards independence, the future of Singapore became a matter of considerable importance and some urgency – the more so because of its great strategic and economic significance. In 1956, the Colonial Secretary Lennox-Boyd told the Cabinet that 'Singapore could never hope to achieve self-government except as part of a larger self-governing whole'.[18] He went on to express the hope that the island would eventually be reunited with the Federation of Malaya. Evidently the considerations which had led to separation less than a decade earlier were now seen as grounds for reunification.

Yet a long delay followed. Five years later, there was strong evidence that Tunku Abdul Rahman was thinking on very similar lines to the British. In October 1961, the Cabinet was told that the existing Government in Singapore had a majority of only one in the Legislative Assembly,[19] and there was real fear of a communist takeover in the near future. The Tunku was anxious to secure a merger of Singapore with Malaya, but 'would be unwilling to contemplate such a merger unless it could include the British Borneo territories whose non-Chinese populations would help to maintain the racial balance against the Chinese population of Singapore'.

An arrangement by which Malaya, Singapore, the two British Borneo colonies and possibly the Protectorate of Brunei could all be united in a Federation would have another advantage too. No doubt the Borneo colonies would one day seek to break the British link, and their future when that day came was by no means assured. Neither of them could hope to resist from its own resources the possible cupidity of outsiders. So the idea of an extended Malayan Federation – 'Malaysia' – gained widespread support.

Opposition to the 'Malaysia' proposal was nevertheless considerable in all the countries concerned. In Malaya itself, some parties were critical. In Singapore, it was fought fiercely by the communists. Opinion in Sarawak and North Borneo was deeply divided. In the end, however, the Borneo dependencies and Singapore all produced large majorities in favour of inclusion. Only oil-rich Brunei resisted all blandishments. The attempt to establish 'Malaysia' involved considerable international problems as well. In the early 1960s, the Indonesian Government was in an expansionist mood. The Dutch were driven from West Irian, their last possession in the archipelago, in 1962. Later in the same year, Indonesia sparked off a revolt – unsuccessful as it proved – in Brunei. In April 1963, North Borneo and Sarawak were both invaded by Indonesians, but these ventures were also unsuccessful.

The United Nations, not wholly convinced by any of the competing claimants, conducted its own investigations in Sarawak and North Borneo and reached the conclusion that most of the people in both favoured inclusion in Malaysia. So, after much 'acrimonious haggling over finance, taxation and trade',[20] the new Federation of Malaysia was finally brought into existence on 16 September 1963. But the link with Singapore, which was originally a major object of the whole exercise, did not last long. Tensions, partly ethnic and partly economic, soon escalated. There was a personality clash between the Tunku and the abrasive Lee Kuan Yew, Prime Minister of Singapore. In the end, Lee was summoned to Kuala Lumpur and told that Singapore would be ejected from Malaysia. Despite attempts of the British and Australian authorities to dissuade them, the Malaysian parliament confirmed the separation. In these remarkable circumstances, Singapore became an independent member of the Commonwealth in August 1965. Fears that the communists would take power there were not realised.

*

There remained many smaller territories which were still British dependencies. A comprehensive review of the current situation and likely future developments in such places was submitted to the Prime Minister by a committee of senior civil servants in May 1957.[21] The overall view is illuminating:

> There are numerous small Colonial territories, practically all islands, scattered around the surface of the globe ... . Some of these Colonies have strategic value, either to us, the Commonwealth or NATO, e.g. Bermuda and Fiji. Some are dollar earners (e.g. Bermuda and the Bahamas). Some have frankly no material value to the United Kingdom as far as we can see today and call for (usually very small) assistance from U.K. funds, e.g. St Helena. Practically none could hope to maintain themselves with a stable administration if we withdrew.

The committee took a very bleak view of what would happen in some of them in the event of British withdrawal. In Fiji there was a very large immigrant population of Indians. Unless New Zealand was prepared to take over responsibility, the committee reported, 'there is the likelihood of strife between the Fijians and Indians and the lapse of the territory into chaos'. The Solomon Islands 'would revert to a primitive form of existence with little prospect of advance'. The Gilbert Islands (now Kiribati) 'would relapse into primitive savagery with little hope of advance unless another civilised country assumed the administration' – a view, incidentally, from which the Resident Commissioner sharply dissented. Such reservations, however, did not greatly inhibit the drive towards independence in all three cases, and even in other islands like Nauru which appeared even less likely to be able to assume an international identity.

11
Seeking a Role

In 1962, the former American Secretary of State, Dean Acheson reflected that Britain 'has lost an Empire and has not yet found a role'.[1] The quest for a new role had already commenced long before Acheson spoke – indeed, it began at a time when a good deal of the British Empire was still not lost. In some respects the quest was a response to the actual, or incipient, loss of Empire; in other respects it probably accelerated the loss of Empire – or at least the loss of British influence in places which had once formed part of the Empire, and were still part of the Commonwealth.

But even after Acheson spoke, the idea of some sort of continuing Imperial role for Britain was not completely abandoned.[2] During the 1960s, there was much talk of a 'role' or 'presence', East of Suez. Not only did Britain retain responsibilities in Southern Arabia until 1967, but she had obligations towards the little states or sheikhdoms of the Persian Gulf and for the defence of Malaysia and Singapore. There was risk of very serious trouble with Indonesia, and at one point 68,000 British servicemen were present in the area. But an economic downswing, which culminated in devaluation of the pound in November 1967, was followed in the next year by a decision to withdraw from most defence responsibilities East of Suez. This 1968 decision, in the words of two recent authors, 'effectively marked the end of Britain as a global military and imperial power'.[3] A lasting legacy of this interest in 'East of Suez' was provided by the establishment of a new British dependency, known as the British Indian Ocean Territories, formed by the grouping of some island

dependencies of Mauritius and the Seychelles, in order to provide
defence facilities for the British and United States Governments.

In the 1950s and 1960s, many people reached the view that the
proper role for Britain was as one of the leading partners in some
European grouping. At the Messina Conference of mid-1955, the
'six' members of the European Coal and Steel Community – France,
Italy, West Germany, Belgium, the Netherlands and Luxembourg –
decided to initiate plans to integrate their economies much more
closely than in the past. The discussions which supervened would
eventually produce the European Economic Community, or
'Common Market'.

The United Kingdom was invited to participate in the plans at an
early stage. When the matter was raised in Eden's Cabinet at the end
of June, two radically different currents of thought could be perceived,[4] both of which have existed ever since in all parties. One
view, represented by Foreign Secretary Harold Macmillan, considered that Britain should enter discussions on the same footing as the
'six'; the other view, represented by Chancellor of the Exchequer
R.A. Butler, was much more sceptical, holding that Britain should
participate only as an observer. There was no formal split, but in
practice Britain remained on the sidelines.

In the course of 1957, the European 'six' pushed swiftly towards
the formation of the EEC, without British participation. Two years
later, however, negotiations took place which led to the establishment of a body known as the European Free Trade Association,
which included the United Kingdom, Austria, Denmark, Norway,
Portugal, Sweden and Switzerland. EFTA aimed at free trade between
the member countries, but – unlike the EEC – did not require them
to pursue common trading policies towards the outside world.

In the first few years after its formation, the EEC was seen to be
making rapid advances, while the British economy appeared to be
relatively stagnant. There were discussions in many quarters about
whether Britain should seek to join the EEC after all. But there were
many problems involved. One of the most serious was that 'we
should have to abandon our special economic relationship with the
Commonwealth, including free entry for Commonwealth goods
and the preferential system, and should instead be obliged to discriminate actively against the Commonwealth'.[5] To abandon
Imperial, or Commonwealth, Preference was one thing; to discrimi-

nate against the Commonwealth in favour of a group of European countries was a very different thing.

In the middle of 1961, ministers were despatched to Commonwealth countries to discuss matters with representatives of the various governments. There was general agreement in those countries that the decision must lie with Britain; but there were also profound apprehensions about the likely consequences if she joined. Nobody showed any positive enthusiasm.

Duncan Sandys visited Australia, New Zealand and Canada. Although the 'old Commonwealth' showed concern about changes in trading arrangements,

> they were even more concerned about its political implications. They feared that an economic union between the United Kingdom and the other countries of Western Europe would lead in one way or another to a political union which must weaken the Commonwealth relationship. Canada also feared that this would draw her increasingly into the economic and political orbit of the United States.[6]

Peter Thorneycroft, who visited the self-governing Commonwealth countries in Asia, reported similar apprehensions. In India there had also been 'some fear lest the emergence of a powerful economic and political union might retard the industrial advance of the under-developed countries'.[7] John Hare reported that Ghana, Nigeria and Sierra Leone felt 'suspicion of the neo-colonial character of the EEC'.[8] Iain Macleod was not able personally to visit the Colonies, but drew much evidence from others, which showed that

> no colonial territory was enthusiastic about the idea. Many probably would prefer us not to, though they did not feel it was for them to say so. British Guiana, British Honduras and Hong Kong have said openly that they would prefer the United Kingdom not to join the Six.[9]

Edward Heath had talks with both Greek and Turkish leaders in Cyprus, and reported that 'they believed that for the United Kingdom to join the EEC would weaken the political and economic cohesion of the Commonwealth, which they would deplore'.[10] They

also considered that the effect of the resulting political and economic changes 'would be to increase support for the Communist
Party, now numbering between 30–40% of the electorate'.

In spite of these bleak reports from Commonwealth countries, the
Cabinet agreed in July 1961 that Britain should seek admission to
the EEC, though the application was said to be 'for the purpose of
enabling negotiations to take place with a view to ascertaining
whether the special needs of the United Kingdom ... other
Commonwealth countries ... [and] other members of EFTA could be
met'.[11] Edward Heath was put in charge of the negotiations from the
British side.

As discussions proceeded, it became clear that different
Commonwealth countries would be affected in very different ways
if Britain joined. India and Ceylon, who both exported a great deal
of tea to Britain, might well benefit, for the EEC countries were
apparently prepared to remove their own 18 per cent duty on tea.
This meant that exports to Britain would be unharmed, while new
markets in EEC countries might open.[12] It was soon recognised that
'the central problem was the treatment of temperate agricultural
products from the older Commonwealth countries'.[13]

This did not mean that all Asian Commonwealth countries, still less
the African countries, were reconciled. When the Commonwealth
Prime Ministers met in September 1962, it was evident that 'the
general attitude ... had so far been more critical than had been
expected'.[14] There was 'widespread apprehension that, if we joined the
Community, our links with the Commonwealth would be seriously
weakened'. As predicted, the problems of countries producing temperate foodstuffs were particularly acute.

Negotiations between Britain and the EEC countries dragged on
throughout 1962. Then, in January 1963, President de Gaulle of
France indicated that the British application was unacceptable. The
British perception was that this was an exclusively French attitude;
but that the French representative 'had ... received instructions to
urge the representatives of the other member countries to rally to
the French point of view under threat that failure to do so would
put the Treaty of Rome itself in jeopardy'.[15]

Enormous damage had been done through the prolonged period
of uncertainty. Producers in Britain, the Commonwealth and EFTA –
indeed, in the EEC itself – had been working for more than a year

on the assumption that British membership was likely. Now all this was apparently over. One cynic commented, 'All that we got out of it was Centigrade.' As for the Commonwealth countries, these negotiations had made many people consider that Britain was abandoning them. They had been forced to seek other markets; and perhaps there could never again be that feeling of confidence which had existed before, most particularly in the 'old Commonwealth'.

The idea that Britain might eventually join the EEC was not abandoned, either by the Conservative Government or by its successor, which took office later in 1964. The Labour Prime Minister Harold Wilson and Foreign Secretary Michael Stewart both clearly contemplated making another British application. At first, the moment was not considered appropriate,[16] but in the spring of 1967 the prospect was again raised.

Several meetings of the Cabinet were held in quick succession to discuss the matter. In the end it was agreed that an application should be made.[17] The Conservative opposition, now headed by the ardently pro-EEC Edward Heath, supported the application, which secured a large majority in the House of Commons.

While the matter was still under active discussion, a Cabinet Memorandum was circulated by Herbert Bowden, Secretary for Commonwealth Affairs. This document not only indicated the likely effects of British membership of the EEC on Commonwealth countries, but it also throws important sidelights on other features of the Commonwealth as it stood in the late 1960s.[18] In some respects, matters were more or less the same as they had been at the time of the earlier approach; in others there were substantial differences.

The minister reflected that the Commonwealth was not exclusively an asset from the British point of view. Britain could no longer 'count on getting her own way'. The Afrasian group, who currently numbered three-quarters of the membership, were disposed to exercise pressure-group tactics, for which the Commonwealth afforded 'a ready-made forum'. Nevertheless, the Commonwealth was seen as – on balance – 'a good thing'. The Memorandum decided that, though there was 'nothing formally incompatible in Britain's joining the EEC and in Britain's continued membership of the Commonwealth ... [yet] in practice ... Britain's membership of the EEC is likely to lead to a diminution of our function as the lynch-pin of the Commonwealth'.

Another Memorandum from the same source developed the economic difficulties which would attend British membership in some detail.[19] Commonwealth countries, it was pointed out, had traditionally exported their produce to the British market, where they enjoyed an average tariff preference of about 12 per cent. Loss of that preference would affect 'old Commonwealth' countries, especially New Zealand, which presented

> the biggest problem. In 1965–66, we took 45% (£168 million) of her total exports – 83% (£50 million) of her mutton and lamb, 86% (£47 million) of her butter and 78% (£16 million) of her cheese.

If Britain joined the EEC without special safeguards, mutton and lamb would face a 20 per cent tariff, while the levies on butter and cheese 'would almost double the cost of New Zealand supplies'. As for Australia, 'we take about one fifth of her exports'. According to Australian Government estimates, if Britain entered the EEC without safeguards, these would drop by £80 million. Canadian trade would also suffer severely. Britain took one-seventh of her exports, and three-quarters of those exports would face tariffs or levies.

In addition to these familiar problems with temperate foodstuffs, another difficulty was recognised which had been less prominent in the earlier discussions. A large number of the smaller countries relied heavily on sugar exports, which were subject to a Commonwealth Sugar Agreement. The effect of Britain joining the EEC without safeguards 'would almost certainly result in the economic collapse of the countries concerned, coupled with industrial unemployment and political unrest'. How far such difficulties could be met by special arrangements was by no means clear.

Although the British application was made in the summer of 1967, it remained in limbo for more than a year and a half. De Gaulle was generally seen as the most severe obstacle. In April 1969, the General at last departed. In June 1970, a few days before a British General Election, it was agreed that new negotiations for Britain's admission should commence later in the month. The election resulted in the return of a Conservative Government headed by Edward Heath.

In the summer of the following year, agreement was reached on most issues affecting the Commonwealth. New Zealand and the sugar producers were more or less appeased, though Australia was somewhat resentful. To what extent any of the Commonwealth countries were truly satisfied must be conjectural; no doubt many of them had long decided that a British Government, of whatever party, was likely to join the EEC sooner or later, and they felt that the arrangements made were about as satisfactory for themselves as could reasonably be hoped.

Britain eventually joined the EEC at the turn of 1972–73. What long-term effect this decision had on the Commonwealth is difficult to quantify. Many adjustments had been made in anticipation long beforehand; others were made gradually over the following several years. Until a Labour Government held a referendum in 1975, there was still a theoretical possibility that Britain might withdraw after all. There can be little doubt, however, that the frequent predictions made even by pro-Marketeers that the overall effect would be to loosen Commonwealth links was fulfilled, though perhaps not quite as dramatically as some had originally feared. Whether Britain had found a new role in Europe remains conjectural to this day. There is not much evidence of the sort of positive enthusiasm for Europe which once existed for the Empire.

*

In her quest for that role in Europe Britain was seeking what was perceived, rightly or wrongly, to be her own interest. But there were other respects in which the gradual collapse of her imperial role required her to play a different part. There were some places where the legacy of Empire proved to be an embarrassment, which Britain could not easily relinquish, but from which she could derive no conceivable advantage. This was particularly the case in Rhodesia and South Africa, from which effective British power had long departed. In both countries, white minorities controlled predominantly black populations. South Africa was undeniably a sovereign state, outside the Commonwealth; but Britain incurred considerable criticism for continuing commercial relations which were, in a sense, a legacy of Empire. Some states, particularly Afrasian states, sought to isolate South Africa completely until 'majority rule' was conceded.

There were particular problems with the sale of weapons and armaments. In the early 1960s, British policy had been to supply South

Africa with ships, naval aircraft and naval ammunition which could be used for protection of sea routes, but to block orders for small arms and related equipment which might be used for riot control.[20] When it looked as if the question of more general sanctions against South Africa would be raised in the United Nations, the British dilemma was well expressed in the Cabinet record of the Foreign Secretary's views:

> To vote in its favour would create a dangerous precedent, particularly as regards our future policy in the case of Southern Rhodesia; while to veto it would be liable to damage our moral standing in the eyes of the world and our relations with the African Commonwealth countries.[21]

After long negotiations, Britain was allowed to escape from that particular hook; but Afrasian pressure for economic sanctions against South Africa continued, and successive governments frequently found themselves in difficulties over the issue.

Not until April 1994 was the problem resolved, when, for the first time, elections in South Africa were held on a truly non-racial basis. The African National Congress secured an overwhelming majority, and Nelson Mandela, surely one of the truly great men of the twentieth century, was elected President. His far-sighted toleration and refusal to support vindictive measures against defeated opponents would prove of crucial importance in enabling South Africa to move remarkably smoothly into a régime very different from any that it had known before. In June 1994, South Africa was welcomed back into the Commonwealth.

Problems over Rhodesia were a good deal more difficult for Britain. Technically, the country was a British colony, and the 'Unilateral Declaration of Independence' of November 1965 was an illegal, possibly a treasonable, act of usurpation. It soon became apparent that the economic sanctions imposed at the end of 1965 were having little effect on ordinary life in Rhodesia.[22] The meeting of Commonwealth Prime Ministers held in September 1966 was dominated by the Rhodesia question. It was reported that a 'particularly disturbing feature of the Meeting had been the establishment of a caucus comprising the African, Asian and West Indian members other than Malaysia and Malawi'.[23] This caucus had conferred separately on

Rhodesia, and then sought to exercise pressure on other members. The upshot was that 'approximately half the Members had been in favour of the use of force', nearly two-thirds had favoured a declaration that no independence would be granted before majority rule; and it was only with 'great patience and firmness that agreement had finally been reached on the terms of the communiqué'. A few more meetings like that could easily destroy the Commonwealth altogether.

The British view was that the possibility of successful negotiations with Rhodesia had not been exhausted. The Government committed itself to proceed with mandatory sanctions, and declared that it would not grant independence before majority rule unless the rebellion was ended by the end of the year.[24] The British Government considered that Ian Smith 'was now seriously concerned about the situation but that he was still in the hands of extremists, however much he might personally wish to rid himself of them'.[25] In the circumstances, 'there was still a chance that Mr Smith might lead the country back to legality'. A meeting was arranged between Wilson and Smith aboard HMS *Tiger*, and for a moment it seemed as if a basis of agreement had perhaps been worked out. It was soon apparent, however, that other members of the Rhodesian régime rejected the proposals.[26] The promise made at the Commonwealth Prime Ministers' Conference was therefore activated, and the British delegate to the United Nations was instructed to propose that mandatory sanctions should be imposed against Rhodesia.[27]

The problem drifted on. There was pressure from Africans, inside and outside the Commonwealth, for armed intervention. Whether this was militarily possible was most dubious;[28] domestic opinion in Britain would assuredly forbid it. In Rhodesia itself there was little sign that sanctions were having a great effect save on the tobacco industry, which was experiencing great difficulty in selling its products. African leaders were kept in captivity; the only perceptible threat to the régime came through guerrilla infiltration from Zambia. Another 'summit' between Wilson and Smith, this time on HMS *Fearless*, proved no more helpful than the previous meeting. The Rhodesian régime became increasingly intransigent. In June 1969, a referendum gave a large majority for the proposal that the country should become a Republic, and a somewhat smaller majority for other constitutional changes, which included the establishment of separate electoral rolls for Africans and Europeans.

No doubt many white Rhodesians hoped for more favourable treatment from a British Government of a different party, but the Conservatives' return in June 1970 did not radically alter the position. A Commission was set up to make proposals for a settlement, whose acceptance had to be conditional on the British Government being satisfied that the terms were acceptable to the Rhodesian people as a whole. The Report was published in November 1971, but the response from Africans was overwhelmingly negative.

For several years more, the Rhodesian problem was unresolved. As time went on, guerrilla activity by alienated black people became increasingly extensive, and operations to counter it imposed a serious and growing burden on the Rhodesian exchequer. In 1976 – by which time another Labour Government was in office – pressure from the United States as well as Britain drove the Smith régime to accept the principle that majority rule must eventually be achieved. This in no way ended the guerrilla warfare, in which casualties continued to mount. In 1977, nearly 3,000 people were killed; in the following year more than 5,000. Part of the difficulty was that no single individual or party, legal or illegal, could be seen as generally representative of black opinion.

In March 1978, an Executive Council, consisting of Ian Smith and three moderate black leaders, was set up. Innumerable negotiations followed. The Labour Government had a most precarious majority in the House of Commons. Anything that might be construed as a concession to the illegal régime in Rhodesia would be sure to produce a revolt among the Government's own followers, and thus was politically impossible. Return of a Conservative Government with a working majority in May 1979 facilitated a compromise, and in November general agreement was reached in London on a constitution for an independent Rhodesia. In the following month, the newly appointed Governor, Lord Soames, arrived in Salisbury (Harare); the illegal Rhodesian parliament ceded power to him; sanctions were lifted; and the country became briefly a British dependency again. Before the year was ended, a cease-fire agreement was reached, ending a war that had cost 20,000 lives.

Although there are big differences between the guerrilla war in Rhodesia and the Mau Mau campaign in Kenya two decades earlier, there are important parallels as well. In both cases, the overwhelming majority of casualties in a long and murderous conflict were not the rebels' ostensible white enemies, but black people whom the rebels were seeking to intimidate. In both cases, the root of the trouble was the fact that white settlers had received the best land many years earlier. This had created in many minds an equation between the colour of people's skin and the possession of natural resources essential for life.

Early in 1980, elections were held for a new Rhodesian parliament. A white voters' roll of 20 seats was monopolised by Ian Smith's Rhodesia Front. Of the 80 common roll seats, 57 were held by Robert Mugabe's Zimbabwe African National Union (ZANU) and most of the remainder by Joshua Nkomo's Zimbabwe African People's Union (ZAPU). Mugabe, as leader of the party which commanded an overall majority, was invited to form a government. In April the country, which was renamed Zimbabwe, became a Republic and was admitted to the Commonwealth.

*

There were three cases where foreign Powers laid claim to British possessions, demanding the right to incorporate that territory in their own country. All were very different from the earlier case of Cyprus, where at one time most of the inhabitants desired *enosis* with Greece. In two cases at least, and perhaps in all three, a large majority of the resident population preferred existing arrangements to the alternative. In all, the outsiders' claim was based on points of international law. Gibraltar became a British possession under the Treaty of Utrecht of 1713. Many years later, there would be much scholarly and diplomatic argument as to the exact title which Spain had conceded to Britain,[29] and whether, in certain circumstances, it might revert *de jure* to Spain. In the nineteenth century, and in both World Wars, Gibraltar was enormously important to Britain as a naval base. The resident population was overwhelmingly of British extraction, although about 5,000 Spaniards worked there, crossing into the colony every day. The existence of a British possession on the Iberian peninsula had been a matter of irritation for Spain for a great many years, but the Spanish complaint was brushed aside in the high days of Empire. It began to attract more attention as the colony's naval importance declined after the Second World War.

The Spanish dictator General Franco was treated as a sort of international pariah for some years after 1945 because of his past association with Hitler and Mussolini, but as the Cold War developed the Western countries were disposed to adopt more 'normal' relations with Spain.[30] In 1964, there was agreement between the British Government and representatives of the Gibraltar legislature, to the effect that the colony should receive an increased measure of self-government. Later in the year, the Spanish authorities began to isolate Gibraltar, in the first instance by imposing much more rigorous control over vehicles crossing the frontier. In October 1966, the customs point at the Spanish frontier town of La Linea was closed. The British Government responded by urging that the whole dispute should be referred to the International Court of Justice: a proposal which their Spanish counterparts rejected.[31]

In 1967, the Spanish authorities prohibited flight by foreign aircraft over parts of their country contiguous with Gibraltar. In good weather, this was no serious impediment, but in bad conditions it made access to Gibraltar difficult. As the dispute deepened, the British Government planned a referendum in Gibraltar on the fundamental question whether it should remain with Britain or revert to Spain. The decision to hold this referendum was roundly condemned by Spain; but when it was held in September of that year, no fewer than 95.46 per cent of the voters went to the poll: 12,138 voted for continued association with the United Kingdom and only 44 favoured reversion to Spain.

In May 1968 the Spanish campaign of isolation went further. The frontier was closed to all traffic, including pedestrians, save for permanent Gibraltar residents and Spaniards with permits to work there. Later in the year, however – notwithstanding the very clear wish of the Gibraltarians – the General Assembly of the United Nations called on Britain to 'terminate the colonial situation in Gibraltar' not later than October 1969. The Spanish then advanced a sort of 'Morton's fork' argument. If Britain failed to 'decolonise' Gibraltar, she would be in defiance of the United Nations; if she did decolonise it, then her claim under the Treaty of Utrecht would lapse.

In May 1969, Britain granted a new constitution to Gibraltar, promising that it would not be transferred against the freely and democratically expressed wishes of the inhabitants. To this the Spanish retorted by closing the frontier entirely. For several years, no major change took place. Then, in November 1975, Franco died, and soon a gradual relaxation of restrictions began. The process was very slow, however, and it was not until the middle 1980s that the matter could be regarded as 'settled' – at least for many years to come.

*

The Falkland Islands were also subject to foreign claims.[32] The islands were uninhabited when the first recorded landing was made by a Briton in 1690. A French settlement was established on East Falkland in 1764, a British settlement on West Falkland in the following year. The islands were intermittently occupied by British, French and Spanish, and were at one point left completely vacant. Who, if anybody, had a legitimate title to the islands in the early nineteenth century must be regarded as a difficult, and unresolved, question of international law. When the Spanish possessions in South America became independent, the predecessor of the present Argentine Republic claimed the Falklands. The British, who disputed this claim, proceeded to occupy them in 1833, and retained possession thereafter. The islands were the scene of an important naval engagement between the British and German fleets in 1914. By the latter part of the twentieth century, the population was around 2,000, nearly all of whom were of British extraction, whose major occupation was sheep rearing.

The dispute between Britain and the Argentine was raised in the United Nations in 1965, and the two countries were invited (perhaps rather unhelpfully) to resolve it between themselves. The first Argentinian attempt to change the status quo by force was in 1966, when eighteen armed members of an extremist group compelled an Argentinian civil airliner to land on the Falklands, and then proceeded to proclaim Argentinian sovereignty.[33] The attempt proved a fiasco and was promptly disavowed by the Argentinian Government, which promised to prosecute the miscreants. They were, however, greeted with considerable enthusiasm by some of their compatriots, who looked upon British occupation of the Falklands rather as many Spaniards viewed British rule in Gibraltar.

A very different kind of Argentinian assault was launched in 1982. The Anglo-Argentinian dispute, which had been rumbling on since 1965, began to escalate late in February, and on 1 March the

Argentinian Foreign Minister warned that his country would seek 'other means' to resolve the matter. Later in the month, about 60 Argentinians, declared to be 'scrap merchants', landed on the Falklands dependency of South Georgia, some 800 miles from the main island group, and hoisted the Argentinian flag. Most were withdrawn shortly afterwards, but some remained behind, and on 30 March the British Foreign Secretary, Lord Carrington, declared that the situation was 'potentially dangerous'. On 2 April, Argentinian troops were landed on the Falkland Islands, rapidly overwhelming the small British force. The Argentinian dictator Leopoldo Galtieri proclaimed the 'recovery' of the Falkland Islands (which he, like most South Americans, preferred to call the Malvinas), and also of South Georgia and the South Sandwich Islands, another Falklands dependency.

A 'task force' of naval vessels, troops, marines and aircraft was mobilised, and proceeded slowly towards the various islands in dispute, via Ascension Island. Meanwhile intense and prolonged diplomatic negotiations took place. The United States was particularly concerned, for Britain was considered its chief ally in Europe and the Argentine its principal ally in South America. The first significant operation was on 25 April, when South Georgia was recovered by British marines. There followed a number of naval and air force operations in and near the Falklands. These included the sinking of the battle-cruiser *General Belgrano* in circumstances which are still the subject of deep controversy. On 21 May, the first British troops were landed on the Falklands. Several weeks of hard fighting followed, culminating in the surrender of Argentine troops at midnight on 14–15 June.

Many factors were involved in this remarkable episode. The Argentinians had a genuine, if contentious, case for ownership of the Falklands, though it is difficult to discern any basis for their claim on the dependencies. They also had a reasonable complaint about the inordinate time which the negotiations had taken. Domestic politics in both countries were much affected by the outcome. Both governments were running through a period of unpopularity when the invasion took place. Victory in an international conflict would doubtless have proved beneficial to Galtieri, while the defeat which took place resulted in his fall almost immediately. In Britain, the popularity of the Conservative Government was greatly enhanced by the nature and effectiveness of the response.

Other considerations were involved as well. The islands had been British for a century and a half, and there was no doubt that virtually all their inhabitants wished them to remain so. To that argument, Argentinian apologists would have retorted that it was hardly surprising that residents in islands which had been populated from Britain would prefer British rule to that of any other country; but the operative question was whether the islands should have been taken by Britain in the first place. More generally, there was a powerful argument for the view that there are many disputed territories in the world, and if one of those territories changed hands through use of force, a most dangerous precedent would be set. Whoever had the better claim to the Falklands, it is surely regrettable that the upshot did not turn on any kind of legal or moral argument, but on the successful use of force. The dead, British and Argentinian together, totalled some 2,000, rather more than the population of the Falklands.[34] The monetary cost to the two countries is difficult to assess, but it must surely be much greater than the value of the islands as real estate.

*

The other British possession whose ownership was challenged in the closing years of the twentieth century was Hong Kong, where the course of events was profoundly different. The circumstances in which Britain acquired control of Hong Kong are not among the most creditable in her imperial annals. Hong Kong island was taken in 1842, as spoils of the 'First Opium War' with China. In 1860, after the 'Second Opium War', another small island, and Kowloon on the Chinese mainland, were added to Hong Kong. By a Convention of 1898, Britain received a 99-year lease from China of the hinterland of Kowloon and many more islands: a territory much larger than the original Colony. In the late twentieth century, the Chinese regarded both 'Opium War' Treaties, and the 1898 Convention too, as dictated arrangements which carried no moral authority at all.

Even as late as 1967, Hong Kong was not a happy place. There were serious internal disturbances and at one point heavy weapons were moved to both sides of the border with China.[35] Corruption was rife in the police and civil service. The political structure of the

Colony remained thoroughly undemocratic. The only governing body with an elected element was the Urban Council, and even in that, half the members were nominated. After the low point in the 1960s, however, the political character of Hong Kong was much improved, while the Colony's economy proved a massive success. By the late 1970s, it was the world's third most important financial centre, after New York and London.[36] The population grew very rapidly, largely as a result of immigration from mainland China, and by the early 1980s was in excess of 5.25 million, more than 98 per cent of whom were ethnic Chinese.

All developments in Hong Kong were overshadowed by the date 1997, when the lease of the New Territories would expire. There was no possibility of a renewal and no prospect of the ceded territories surviving without them. Yet China had much to lose if she were wantonly to destroy the existing fabric. Forty per cent of her foreign exchange passed through Hong Kong, and the existence of a highly prosperous window on the capitalist world was extremely useful to the Chinese Government.

In September 1982, Prime Minister Thatcher visited Peking (now Beijing) for talks with her Chinese counterpart. Discussions at various levels between the two countries were inaugurated, and continued at intervals for a couple of years. In the latter part of 1984, a joint declaration about Hong Kong was produced and was endorsed by the major governmental organs of the two countries over the next few months. The whole colony would be transferred to China when the lease expired on 1 July 1997, but Hong Kong's capitalist system would be preserved for 50 years.

Thereafter, progress was generally smooth. Perhaps the greatest problem, from Britain's point of view, was whether large numbers of Hong Kong residents would seek asylum in the United Kingdom. In practice, provisions were made which averted mass emigration and probably the arrangements governing Hong Kong's transfer proved fairly satisfactory to most residents, including the business community. So, when the last great British colony was transferred to China in the middle of 1997, it was more a formality than a dramatic change. The contrast between the civilised and dignified manner in which the transfer of Hong Kong was handled and the savage altercations which took place over the much less valuable territory of the Falkland Islands is sharp indeed.

After the cession of Hong Kong, little remained of the British Empire. A dozen or more small territories of very limited value are still British dependencies at the beginning of the twenty-first century and a few others are linked to New Zealand or Australia. Such are the vestiges of what had been described, just over a century earlier, as 'a vaster Empire than has been'.

12
Reflections

Although the process of imperial 'liquidation' took place very rapidly, it is impossible to point to some particular event and say that this marked the end of the British Empire. The many people still living who witnessed the process are not conscious of any moment at which some great break took place – as they might remember, for example, the beginning or the ending of the Second World War. Any date which historians set for the end of the British Empire, just like any date they set for the end of the Roman Empire, is arbitrary.

With the priceless gift of after-knowledge, it is obvious today that the British Empire, in the sense in which the term was used in the nineteenth and early twentieth centuries, could only be an ephemeral phenomenon. It was built mainly on sea-power, which happened to be the most important kind of power during the period of its rapid growth, but could not remain so for ever. As for power on dry land, firearms, so useful for quelling 'natives', would not be the monopoly of white men for ever. There was a much better chance that the gentler and more humane institutions which spread with British power – the legal system including the 'Rule of Law', an impartial judiciary, an uncorrupt bureaucracy, the parliamentary system with democratic elections, and so on – would influence people living in British dependencies and encourage them to develop similar institutions of their own. That had already happened in the Dominions before 1914. Might it eventually extend to India and the Colonies as well, turning the British Empire into a great association of independent states freely cooperating with each other, linked by common interest and mutual respect?

In theory at least, this view of future Imperial development was generally accepted long before 1939. In many cases, alas, though not in all, the sanguine hopes would later be disappointed. Part of the problem was the very long time which was necessary for truly democratic institutions to develop. In Britain herself, nearly a century elapsed between the Great Reform Act of 1832 and the establishment of universal adult franchise in 1928; so why should anybody expect other parts of the Empire to develop more rapidly? Again, democracies had been set up in most European countries after 1918; but they usually had shallow roots, and in the course of the 1920s and 1930s most succumbed to dictatorships of one kind or another.

True, all but one of the pre-1939 Dominions had apparently managed to evolve durable democratic institutions with more or less universal franchise, which at first sight suggested that the same process could be repeated elsewhere. But the parallel between those Dominions and most of the other Empire countries was really misleading; for many people living in the Dominions had long been familiar with British-type institutions and could easily apply that experience to the new countries; while in most of the dependencies few people had had such an experience.

The Asian dependencies, and most particularly India, were necessarily among the front-runners in any Imperial development in the direction of independence. From 1917 onwards, it was almost universally accepted that India would become independent one day; and yet, as a recent writer has noted, 'British responses to Indian political demands always came as too-little too-late'.[1] Britain not only failed to act in good time, but sometimes failed to show proper regard for local feeling. The Statutory Commission which was set up in 1927 to consider extensions of the 1919 reforms was evidently designed to produce some common ground among British politicians rather than to satisfy the wishes of Indians. Today it seems almost incredible that the Commission did not include a representative cross-section of Indians. It is almost equally remarkable that the Commission included only one man who at the time would have ranked as a major public figure. Indians could reasonably conclude that they were deemed unworthy to have a part in planning the future of their own country, and that their British rulers considered India was a matter of only second-rate importance by comparison with much smaller countries in Europe.

Nor was there any sense of urgency once the Commission had been set up. Not until eight years later did the relevant legislation find its way onto the Statute Book, and even by the outbreak of war in 1939 the proposed Federal legislature had not come into existence. Similar attitudes continued to be shown in other matters. When a British Viceroy exercised his technical legal right and declared war on Germany in 1939 on India's behalf, he infuriated a great many Indians whose hatred of Nazism and all its works was every bit as strong as his own. Ceylon and Burma were handled rather better in the inter-war period, but again not much sense of urgency could be discerned.

In one vital respect, inter-war India, and to some extent other Asian dependencies as well, differed from most of the Colonies. Many Indians knew Britain well, and were familiar with the work-ings of British institutions. Others who had not actually lived in Britain had had some experience in working a system which had considerable parallels with that in Britain, as members or salaried officials of Indian administrations.

Other British possessions, notably but not exclusively in Africa, were also bound to develop towards independence sooner or later. The overwhelming criticism of British management of those dependencies was, as with India, 'too little, too late'. The tiny band of dedicated colonial officials no doubt did what they could to develop education, to counter poverty and disease and to prepare the local people for eventual self-government; but in all their doings they were held back by the small amount of money and encouragement provided. This, in turn, derived from the disposition by Britons at all levels to take the Empire for granted while they attended to other matters.

The population of the overseas Empire was in the region of ten times the population of the United Kingdom, and considerably greater than that of Europe; so one might have thought that it would constantly loom very large indeed in the minds of the British public and British governments. When something dramatic was happening within the Empire, public attention was certainly riveted on those events. But for most of the time, matters were not like that at all. Thus, in no British General Election after 1900 did imperial questions play a major part.

Another way of looking at the general lack of interest in the Empire is to consider the various offices of state which were concerned with the Empire – the India Office, the Colonial Office, later the Dominions

Office and the Commonwealth Relations Office. For most of the time, none of those offices was regarded by either politicians or public as of major importance. When a politician moved from one of the 'imperial' portfolios to the office of Chancellor of the Exchequer, or Foreign Secretary, or Home Secretary, this was seen universally as a promotion. Again, the Press – 'quality' as well as 'popular' – seldom gave as much attention to an event in the overseas Empire as it gave to some comparable development in Europe – or, for that matter, to a small change in the rate of domestic income tax.

Nor did members of the public know much about the Empire. At the time of Churchill's 'liquidation' speech, most Britons would almost certainly have made a far better shot at labelling the countries on a blank map of Europe than they would have made at labelling the Provinces and major Princely States of India, or the British colonies in Africa.

Again, the Empire, and even the self-governing Dominions, were never fully involved in the major decisions of peace and war. At the time of the 'Munich' crisis of 1938, and at the time of the 'Poland' crisis of 1939, the Dominions were indeed kept informed of what was happening, and their representatives had occasional discussions with the Dominions Secretary (whose rank in the Cabinet was fairly lowly); but nobody who mattered, on government or opposition side, suggested that they had a right to be consulted before action was taken. Nobody considered, for example, that a few major Empire statesmen might have been invited to attend crucial Cabinet meetings, with full rights to participate in discussions and decisions.

The Second World War, and particularly the Japanese aspect of that war, was but the culmination of a long period of general preoccupation with happenings elsewhere. As the last British Governor of Burma reflected, 'Interest was concentrated upon Europe and the East was neglected, with consequences that need no emphasis.'[2] Maybe if Empire statesmen had been present at the crucial deliberations, the course of events would have been radically different. The low priority accorded to Commonwealth opinion continued long after the Second World War. If the British Government had consulted Commonwealth Governments, and particularly Canada, as closely as it consulted the Government of France during the 'Suez' crisis of 1956, vital decisions would probably have been a great deal wiser than they were, and far less damaging to Britain's interests.

While the process of developing self-governing institutions in the Empire proceeded slowly in the pre-1939 period, it suddenly gathered pace when the war was over. In India, one might say, Britain had no choice but to accede to local demands. The eventual upshot was far from ideal, but – granted the situation existing at the end of the war – every credit is due to Mountbatten for extracting Britain honourably from a situation fraught with the most appalling perils.

Whether similar credit is due to those who sounded the Imperial retreat in Africa, or whether it was both possible and desirable to make the withdrawal less abrupt, is not so certain. In the closing period of the 1939–45 war, and in the immediate aftermath, some attention was indeed given to problems of political development in Africa, but even then they had a relatively low priority in the minds of most people, whether politicians or ordinary voters. In any event, it may well have been too late already. Perhaps the surge of ideas and events within the dependent territories was too rapid for anybody to contain.

In many cases, though not all, retreat from Empire was preceded by the development of widespread nationalism in the dependent territories. This took place at different times, at different speeds and in different ways. In India, as has been seen, the process was already advanced long before 1939. Perhaps the same was true in Burma and Ceylon. In most African colonies, nationalism barely existed as a serious force until after 1945, and there were no mass-based indigenous nationalist parties.[3]

In some places, nationalism was almost a forced plant, nurtured by Britain in a hothouse atmosphere in the aftermath of 1945, and there is much to be said for the view that it would have been better to allow it to grow more slowly. Would it have been better for Ghana, and for many other parts of Africa as well, if the pace of development had been moderated rather than stimulated? To give another example, the British in Malaya, conscious of the damage which local disunity had wrought on defence during the Japanese invasion, sought to conjure nationalism into existence, but failed in the attempt. In other places, too, the creation of 'nationalism' was a difficult job for the British to perform when they wished to do so. How could one persuade the Muslims of northern Nigeria that they had a common 'nationality' with the Christians of the south, when they were so very different not only in religion but in many other ways, and when 'Nigeria' itself was a recent European creation? How could one persuade the autochthonous people of Fiji that they belonged to the same 'nation' as the great number of Indian immigrants who had arrived in comparatively recent times?

Almost everywhere, one might say, 'nationalism' was a concept which developed far more easily among literate middle-class people than among the masses.[4] Action by the masses was often turbulent, taking the form of riots or strikes; but it was usually in protest against some visible cause of grievances, such as hunger, poverty, landlessness or bad working conditions, not in order to encourage the transfer of government to indigenous people. Local leaders – whether chiefs or intellectuals – were sometimes willing to indoctrinate the masses with nationalist ideas; but they were often conscious that nationalism might prove a two-edged sword.[5]

In the end, did the British Empire fall, or was it pushed?[6] One is led to the conclusion that it was a bit of both. Nationalism, led by the indigenous middle classes, did indeed force the British out of India and played some part elsewhere in Asia; but the British withdrawal from Africa took place for very different reasons. Around the mid-1950s the British Government, and probably most ordinary Britons as well, had become weary of Empire, and were willing, even anxious, to depart – always provided that domestic living standards did not suffer. That is not to say that the decolonisation process always took place at exactly the pace the British wished. Once the Gold Coast received full independence, it could only be a matter of time – and not much time at that – before all the other African colonies went the same way, whether or not they were ready for it. Soon the French colonies in Africa were also advancing rapidly towards independence, and a 'positive feedback' developed. People who had had no experience of self-government found themselves, within a very few years, completely independent.

The consequences in the years that followed independence were to a large extent predictable. It was impossible to return to the values and institutions of the societies which had existed before the British arrived; but not enough had been done to prepare for the very different kinds of society which would develop after the British departure. In many places, not only were the people with the education and experience necessary to give future leadership few in number, but there were even fewer people who could subject them to responsible criticism. Those who took power were exposed to all the temptations of megalomania and corruption. A few of the leaders who took office in the immediate aftermath of independence were great enough and wise enough to resist those temptations. All too often, the aftermath of empire was marked by incompetent and venal civil governments which alternated with brutal military dictatorships.

The experience of Britain's former African colonies in the couple of decades or so which followed independence brings those points out sharply. In Ghana, there was an army coup in 1966, but in 1969 a President was again elected. Another army coup followed in 1972. The military régime fell to another coup in 1978. In Nigeria, there were major clashes between Ibo and Hausa in 1966, in which thousands were killed, and a military government was then set up. In the following year civil war supervened, and Ibos declared an independent Republic of Biafra in the former Eastern region. Perhaps this was hardly surprising, for it was in that region that very valuable oil deposits were currently being developed. In 1970 Biafra was conquered; thereafter military government and corrupt civilian rule alternated in Nigeria for years to come. In Sierra Leone the local military overthrew the civilian government in 1967, but were ousted in the following year. In 1978, the country became a one-party state. Another military régime was set up in 1992. Even little Gambia had troubles of its own, including an attempted coup in 1981; while the question of the country's relations with Senegal still appears unresolved.

Kenya was more fortunate after independence. The presidency of Jomo Kenyatta, which lasted until his death in 1978, provided the political stability which enabled economic growth to take place. Four years after his death, however, there was an unsuccessful attempt at an army coup. Tanzania also profited from a long period of rule by a widely respected figure who had played a major part in his country's move towards independence, for Julius Nyerere remained President until his retirement in 1985. In the late 1970s, however, Tanzania experienced serious trouble from Uganda, whose history since independence had been much more turbulent. President Mutesa of Uganda was pushed out in 1966 by Obote, who was himself overthrown in 1971 by a military coup led by the infamous Idi Amin. In 1978, Amin invaded Tanzania, and in the following year Tanzanian forces retaliated, deposing Amin in the process. In 1980, Obote again became President, but another military coup followed a few years later.

So in most African countries which had formed part of the British Empire, the political aftermath to independence was very different from what the optimists, British and African alike, had anticipated in the middle of the twentieth century. The economic aftermath was often disappointing as well, for political instability discourages investment. In human terms, this has often meant very bleak prospects for people living in the former colonies. To this day, life expectancy in Sierra Leone is one of the very lowest in the world. Such experiences were not peculiar to former British colonies. Referring to Africa, Paul Johnson noted that 'By the early 1980s, all the newly independent states, with the exception of the Ivory Coast, Kenya and the three oil-bearing territories, Algeria, Libya and Nigeria, were poorer than under the colonial system'.[7]

Yet the picture is not all gloom. Some of the former African dependencies are now, to all appearances, settling down to a much more stable political system, although in many places the economic and social problems are immense. The process by which South Africa moved from apartheid to racial equality, at least in a legal sense, was astonishingly smooth. In a different part of the world, India has contrived with great skill to preserve the structure of a democracy with deeply entrenched civil liberty.

Sometimes the ethnic problems of a former dependency were complicated by special difficulties for which Britain was largely responsible. Where that happened, the trouble was not primarily due to any faults of the decolonisation process, but to policies which had been followed long before. The problems of Kenya and Zimbabwe, where much of the best land had been taken by white settlers, have been considered. In some places, the incomers were not Britons at all, and the problem was not directly related to land ownership in the dependent country. Indians or Chinese were imported to do jobs which neither Europeans nor the original inhabitants were willing to perform. These 'invasions' sometimes took place on a huge scale in the high days of Empire, while little was done to integrate the incomers with the existing society. Malaya was a striking example; while in places as scattered as Guyana, Fiji and Zanzibar, Asian incomers were present in such enormous numbers that in the last days of Empire political parties were defined largely by race.

The British Empire has left a durable legacy in the form of the Commonwealth. The great majority of territories which were once included in the British Empire are still part of the Commonwealth. Several important members left the Commonwealth, but later saw fit to return. In 1995, Mozambique, which had never formed part of the British Empire, and Cameroons, of which only a small part had belonged, were welcomed as members. Evidently the peoples of the many countries concerned perceive advantages in the Commonwealth association. David McIntyre has recently observed:[8]

> If the Head of the Commonwealth and the biennial Heads of Government meetings represent the tip of an iceberg, below the line of visibility the meetings of senior officials and ministers, the professional conferences, the organising work of the Secretariat, Foundation, Fund for Technical Cooperation and Commonwealth of Learning, as well as the myriad activities of the professional and sporting bodies represent some of the more tangible advantages of membership.

The even closer link of what used to be called 'Dominion status', with the Queen as Head of State, is still retained by a considerable number of countries: not only those populated by people of British stock, but also most of the West Indies. Australia, whose present population contains a very high proportion of people from continental Europe and from Asia, decided as recently as 1999 that it was worth retaining that particular link.

Neither monarchical nor republican institutions provide any guarantee of civil liberties, and some countries have been permitted to remain members of the Commonwealth while sustaining régimes that violate what most people would consider to be fundamental human rights. Perhaps it will one day become possible to insist that the perceived advantages of membership are conditional on high standards of behaviour by the governments of Commonwealth countries.

Notes

1 Zenith

1. George Orwell, *The Road to Wigan Pier* (1937; London, 1986), p. 148.
2. See John Darwin, *Britain and Decolonisation*, p. 30.
3. John W. Coll, in OHBE IV, p. 232.
4. Attlee to Bevin, 2 January 1947. *Transfer of Power* IX, p. 245.
5. Robert MacGregor Dawson, *The Development of Dominion Status 1900–1936*, p. 5.
6. Dawson, *op. cit.*, p. 18.
7. War Cabinet 172, 29 June 1917. CAB 23/3.
8. War Cabinet 214, 14 August 1917. CAB 23/3.
9. See Alfred Draper, *Amritsar: The Massacre that Ended the Raj*.
10. Viceroy's telegram cited in War Cabinet 556, 14 April 1919. CAB 23/10.
11. Cab. 49(22) 15 September 1922. CAB 23/31.
12. Council of Ministers 30 September 1922. CAB 23/39.
13. Council of Ministers 19 September 1922. CAB 23/39.

2 Uneasy Peace

1. Cabinet 58(26) 17 November 1926. CAB 23/53.
2. 260 H.C.Deb. 5.s, 326 *et seq.* 24 November 1931.
3. P.J. Cain and A.G. Hopkins, *British Imperialism: Crisis and Deconstruction 1914–1990*, p. 226.
4. Werner Schlote, *British Overseas Trade from 1700 to the 1930s*, pp. 165, 167.
5. See A.N. Porter and A.J. Stockwell, *British Imperial Policy ...*, I, 17.
6. Judith M. Brown, *Modern India: The Origins of an Asian Democracy*, p. 236.
7. Brown, *op. cit.*, p. 237.
8. C.P. 187(27). 12 July 1927. CAB 24/187.
9. Cain and Hopkins, *op. cit.*, pp. 188–9.
10. R.F. Holland, *European Decolonization 1918–1981*, pp. 6–7.
11. Cabinet 33(30) 24 June 1930. CAB 23/64.
12. Cabinet 35(32) 15 June 1932. CAB 23/71.
13. Cabinet 1(37) 13 January 1937. CAB 23/87.
14. Cabinet 68(32) 21 December 1932. CAB 23/73.
15. H.L. 5s. vol. cxxv. 3 December 1942, 408 *et seq.*

3 Coming of War

1. Review of Imperial Defence ... 26 February 1937. C.P.73(37). CAB 24/268.
2. Cabinet 15(38) 22 March 1938. CAB 23/93; CAB 53/10; 53/37.

3. See Hankey memorandum MO(36)10, ff. 161–9, 21 December 1936. CAB 63/51. Cited in BDEE ser. A, vol. 1, I, 82.
4. PREM 1/242, especially Memo. of September 1938, fo. 72 *et seq.* and of 19 September 1938, fo. 51 *et seq.*
5. Ibid.
6. C. te Water Memo. 27 September 1938. PREM 1/242, fo. 27.
7. Tweedsmuir to Chamberlain, 27 October 1938. PREM 1/242, fos. 7–8.
8. Keith Jeffrey, in OHBE IV, p. 307.
9. See also Jeffrey, *op. cit.*, p. 309.
10. W.M. 58(39) 24 October 1939. CAB 65/1.
11. Ibid.
12. Churchill to Halifax, 22 October 1939. FO 800/310, cited by Martin Gilbert, *Winston S. Churchill*, vol. VI, p. 67.
13. W.M. 58(39) 24 October 1939. CAB 65/1.
14. Marquis of Zetland, *The Indian Federation.* C.P. 169(39), 27 July 1939. CAB 24/288.
15. W.M. 29(39) 27 September 1939. CAB 65/1.
16. Keith Jeffrey, in OHBE IV, p. 311, fn., citing Manzoor Ahmad.
17. W.M. 70(39) 4 November 1939. CAB 65/2.
18. Ibid.
19. W.M. 121(39) 21 December 1939. CAB 65/2.
20. W.M. 89(40) 12 April 1940. CAB 65/6.
21. W.M. 279(40) 29 October 1940. CAB 65/9.
22. W.M. 293(40) 21 November 1940. CAB 65/10.
23. W.M. 303(40) 10 December 1940. CAB 65/10.

4 The Impact of Japan

1. Hankey minute, 5 April 1933. PREM 1/152, BDEE 1, I, 65.
2. Winston Churchill, *The Second World War*, vol. 3, p. 157.
3. Churchill to Attlee, 7 January 1942. *Transfer of Power* I, p. 14.
4. W.M. 16[42] 5 February 1942. CAB 65/25.
5. W.M. 31[42] 9 March 1942. CAB 65/29.
6. Linlithgow to Amery, 13 August 1943. *Transfer of Power* IV, p. 169.
7. W.M. (43)131, 24 September 1943. CAB 65/35.
8. Hugh Toye, *The Springing Tiger*.
9. W.M. (45)56 30 April 1945. CAB 65/52.
10. W.P. (44)299 7 June 1944: CAB 66/50; W.M. 77(44), 13 June 1944: CAB 65/42.

5 Aftermath

1. C.P. (45) 281, 14 September 1945. CAB 129/4.
2. Cunningham to Wavell, 27 September 1943. *Transfer of Power* VI, p. 546.

3. Wavell to Pethick-Lawrence, 27 November 1945. *Transfer of Power* VI, p. 532.
4. C.M. 65 (46) 5 July 1946. CAB 128/6.
5. C.P. (46) 456. Indian Policy (Attlee) 24 December 1946. CAB 129/15.
6. C.M. 4 (47) 8 January 1947. CAB 128/11 Wavell's diary indicates other possibilities as well, but does not suggest that the Viceroy took them very seriously.
7. C.P. (46) 456.
8. C.M. 104 (46) 10 December 1946. CAB 128/8.
9. C.M. (47) 18 February 1947. CAB 128/11.
10. Mountbatten to Attlee, 20 December 1946. *Transfer of Power* IX, p. 396.
11. Philip Ziegler, *Mountbatten: The Official Biography*, p. 359.
12. Report, 2 April 1947. *Transfer of Power* X, p. 90.
13. C.M. 50 (47) 23 May 1947. CAB 128/10.
14. Madras Resident, 13 July 1947. *Transfer of Power* XII, p. 93.
15. Attlee to Bevin, 3 January 1947. *Transfer of Power* IX, p. 446.
16. W.P. (42) 346, cited in Burma I, 1.
17. Duncan-Smith to Amery, 25 July 1945. Burma I, 384.
18. C.M. 58 (47) 1 July 1947. CAB 128/10.
19. C.P. (47) 144, Ceylon constitution (Greenwood). 2 May 1947. CAB 129/18.
20. C.P. (47) 147. 5 May 1947. CAB 129/18.
21. W.P. (44) 258, 18 May 1944: CAB 66/50; W.M. 70 (44) 31 May 1944: CAB 65/42.
22. C.M. 103 (46), 5 December 1946. CAB 128/6.
23. C.M. 59 (47) 3 July 1947. CAB 128/10.
24. C.C. 10 (51). 22 November 1951. CAB 128/23.
25. N.J. Ryan, *The Making of Modern Malaysia* ..., pp. 213–15.
26. C.M. (48) 67. 28. October 1948; C.M. (48) 71, 12 November 1948. Confidential Annexes. CAB 128/14.
27. C.M. (49) 29. 27 April 1949. CAB 128/15.
28. David McIntyre, in OHBE IV, p. 696.
29. CAB 129/31/1. Attlee, 30 December 1948. CP(48)307.

6 Ottoman Succession

1. The word 'Protectorate' was used, though in a different sense from that in which it was applied in other parts of the Empire.
2. War Cabinet 245, 4 October 1917. CAB 23/4.
3. War Cabinet 261, 31 October 1917. CAB 23/4.
4. War Cabinet 245, 4 October 1917. CAB 23/4.
5. War Cabinet 227, 3 September 1917. CAB 23/4.
6. War Cabinet 261, 31 October 1917. CAB 23/4. In 1917, the War Cabinet was very small, and neither Balfour nor Montagu was a member, although both were sometimes invited to share in its deliberations.
7. War Cabinet 601, 29 July 1919. CAB 23/11.

8. Figures based on Royal Institute of International Affairs, *Great Britain and Palestine 1915–1945*, p. 61.
9. Ibid., p. 13.
10. John Darwin, *Britain and Decolonisation*, p. 53.
11. *Annual Register* 1934, p. 276.
12. Cmd. 6019, 17 May 1939.
13. Cabinet 38(45) 4 October 1945. CAB 128/1.
14. See P.W. Holt and M.W. Daly, *A History of the Sudan from the Coming of Islam to the Present Day*. 4th edn.
15. Cabinet 76(46) 1 August 1946. CAB 28/6.
16. C.M. 12(47) 27 January 1947. CAB 128/9.
17. C.M. 30 (45) Confidential Annex. 11 September 1945. CAB 128/3.
18. C.M. (46) 38. 29 April 1946. CAB 128/5.
19. C.M. 6 (47) 15 January 1947. (Confidential Annexes) CAB 128/11.
20. C.M. 76 (47) 20 September 1947. CAB 128/10.

7 The Road to Suez

1. C.P. (51) 94. 26 March 1951. CAB 128/45.
2. B.R. Mitchell, *International Historical Statistics: Africa, Asia and Oceania, 1750–1993*, 3rd edn, 1998, gives crude oil production for 1950: Iran, 32,259,000 metric tons; Saudi Arabia, 26,649,000; Kuwait, 17,291,000. No other Middle Eastern country came within 10,000,000 metric tons of the last figure.
3. C.P. (51) 257. 26 September 1951. CAB 129/47.
4. C.P. (51) 244. 7 September 1951. CAB 129/47.
5. '...*omnium consensu capax imperii nisi imperasset*', *Histories*, i, p. 49.
6. C. (55) 70. 14 March 1955. CAB 129/74.
7. Anthony Eden, *Memoirs III: Full Circle* (1960), p. 220.
8. C.C. (55) 24. 15 March 1955. CAB 128/28.
9. C. (55) 70. 14 March 1955. CAB 129/74.
10. See Harold Macmillan, *Tides of Fortune, 1945–55*, pp. 631–2.
11. Anthony Nutting, *No End of a Lesson*, p. 29.
12. Selwyn Lloyd, *Suez 1956*, pp. 70–1.
13. Lloyd, ibid., p. 71.
14. Lloyd, ibid., p. 72.
15. Eden, *op. cit.*, p. 426.
16. Ibid., p. 429.
17. Nutting, *op. cit.*, p. 55.
18. C.M. (56)54. 27 July 1956. CAB 128/30/2.
19. *Idem*.
20. C.C. (56)56. 1 August 1956. CAB 128/30/2.
21. Nutting, *op. cit.*, p. 61.
22. C.C. (56)64. 11 September 1956. CAB 128/30/2.
23. C.C. (56)68. 3 October 1956. CAB 128/30/2.

24. CRO to High Commissioners (for PMs) Canada, New Zealand, South Africa 30 October 1956. PREM 11/1096 fo. 168.
25. C.M. (56)71. 18 October 1956. CAB 128/30/2.
26. C.C. (56) 71. 18 October 1956. CAB 128/30/2.
27. C.C. (56) 72. 23 October 1956. CAB 128/30/2.
28. C.C. (56) 74. 25 October 1956. CAB 128/30/2.
29. Menzies to Eden 1 November 1956. PREM 11/1096 fo. 142.
30. HC to CRO 1 November 1956.
31. Holland to Eden 1 November 1956. PREM 11/1096 fo. 124.
32. HC to CRO 31 October 1956. PREM 11/1096 fo. 165.
33. HC to CRO 1 November 1956. PREM 11/1096 fo. 128.
34. HC to CRO 31 October 1956. PREM 11/1096 fo. 160.
35. HC to CRO 1 November 1956. PREM 11/1096 fo. 103.
36. CRO to HC South Africa 3 November 1956. PREM 11/1096 fo. 51.
37. HC to CRO 31 October 1956. PREM 11/1096 fo. 153.
38. St Laurent to Eden via HC/CRO. PREM 11/1096 fo. 121.
39. HC to CRO 5 November 1956. PREM 11/1096 fo. 54.
40. HC to CRO 5 November 1956. PREM 11/1096 fo. 41.
41. HC to CRO 5 November 1956. PREM 11/1096 fo. 54.
42. Nutting, *op. cit.*, p. 105.

8 Colonial Africa

1. A. Marshall Macphee, *Kenya*, pp. 73–4.
2. See, for example, Cmd. 7433, 1948.
3. C.M. (49) 21. 21 March 1949. CAB 128/15.
4. Nicholas White, *Decolonisation*, p. 9.
5. C(55) 43. 11 February 1955. CAB 129/73.
6. Nigel Fisher, *Iain Macleod*, p. 142.
7. See, for example, David McIntyre, *British Decolonization*, p. 47.
8. See W.E.F. Ward, *A History of Ghana*, pp. 324 *et seq.*
9. D. George Boyce, *Decolonisation...*, p. 120.
10. C.M. (56) 64. 11 September 1956. CAB 128/30/2.
11. C(53) 122. 8 April 1953. CAB 129/60.
12. McIntyre, *op. cit.*, pp. 47–8.
13. See, e.g., Macpherson to Lloyd, 16 March 1953. BDEE A3, II, 191.
14. C.C. (57) 42. 22 May 1957. CAB 128/31/2.
15. C.C. (57) 42. 22 May 1957. CAB 128/31/2.
16. Boyce, *op. cit.*, p. 201.
17. Harry A. Gailey, *A History of the Gambia*, p. 186; Macleod to Macmillan 6 December 1960. PREM 11/4683.
18. C.C. (61) 2. 24 January 1961. CAB 128/35/1.
19. O.S. to Home, 17 April 1964. PREM 11/4683.
20. See Gailey, *op. cit.*, p. 204.
21. 608 HC Deb. 5s, 29 June 1959, cols. 17–19 (Written answers).
22. C.C. (61) 63. 16 November 1961. CAB 128/35/2.

23. C.C. (62) 26. 5 April 1962. CAB 128/36/1.
24. C.C. (62) 22. 20 March 1962. CAB 128/36/1.
25. C.C. (62) 44. 5 July 1962. CAB 128/36/2.
26. C.M. (63) 7. 21 November 1963. CAB 128/38/1.
27. Phores Mutibwa, *Uganda since Independence*, gives some very useful information about the earlier period, as well as the main subject of the study.
28. Macleod to Macmillan, 31 May 1960. PREM 11/3240 fo. 8 *et seq.*
29. McIntyre, *op. cit.*, p. 50.
30. See Rodger Yeager, *Tanzania: An African Experiment.*
31. McIntyre, *op. cit.*, p. 49.
32. Macleod to Macmillan, 31 May 1960. PREM 11/3240 fo. 8 *et seq.*
33. C.C. (62) 26. 5 April 1962. CAB 128/36/1.
34. C.M. (64) 21. 9 April 1964. CAB 128/38/2.
35. See I.M. Lewis, *A Modern History of Somalia.*
36. C.M. (55) 29. 26 August 1955. CAB 128/29.

9   Southern Africa

1. A summary of contemporary attitudes is given in *Liberal Magazine* 1909, 491–7.
2. C.C. (60) 20. 24 March 1960. CAB 128/34.
3. C.C. (60) 34. 2 June 1960. CAB 128/34.
4. C.C. (61) 13. 16 March 1961. CAB 128/35/1.
5. Letter to Asquith, 18 November 1897, cited in Robert Blake, *A History of Rhodesia,* p. 114.
6. C.C. (51) 7. 15 November 1951. CAB 128/23.
7. Blake, *op. cit.*, p. 284.
8. Blake, *op. cit.*, p. 296.
9. C.C. (57) 76. 28 October 1957. CAB 128/31/2; C.C. (58) 7. 20 January 1958. CAB 128/32/1.
10. C.C. (60) 6. 9 February 1960. CAB 128/34.
11. C.C. (60) 10. 18 February 1960. CAB 128/34.
12. C.C. (61) 3. 31 January 1961. CAB 128/35/1.
13. C.C. (62) 64. 29 October 1962. CAB 128/36/2.
14. J.R.T. Wood, *The Welensky Papers,* p. 1218.
15. C.C. (63) 55. 20 September 1963. CAB 128/37.
16. See discussion of these Acts in Wood, *op. cit.*
17. C.C. (63) 33. 21 May 1963. CAB 128/37.
18. Blake, *op. cit.*, p. 359.
19. C.M. (64) 14. 25 February 1964. CAB 128/38/2.
20. C.C. (65) 6. 1 February 1965. CAB 128/39/1. A detailed report of the meeting is given in PREM 13/174.
21. C.C. (65) 58. 9 November 1965. CAB 128/39/3.
22. C.C. (65) 59. 10 November 1965. CAB 128/39/3.
23. C.C. (65) 60. 11 November 1965. CAB 128/39/3.
24. I. Goldblatt, *History of South-West Africa...,* pp. 221; 226–7.

25. See C (51) 21. 19 November 1951. CAB 129/48.
26. C (51) 21. 19 November 1951. CAB 129/48.
27. 472 H.C. Deb. 5s., 285 *et seq.* 8 March 1950.
28. C.C. (51) 10, 11, 22. 27 November 1951. CAB 128/23.

10 Smaller Colonies

1. C.C. (54) 57. 27 August 1954.CAB 128/27/2.
2. C.C. 53 (54) 26 July 1954. CAB 128/27/2.
3. C.C. 7 (59) 12 February 1959. CAB 128/33.
4. C.C. (60) 47. 28 July 1960. CAB 128/34.
5. Luce to Barnes, 27, 28 March 1958. BDEE A4, I, 557 *et seq.*
6. J.O. Wright to Home, 8 April 1964. BDEE A4, I, 639; C.C. 59 (62), 9 October 1962. CAB 128/36/2.
7. Amery, 10 March 1959. BDEE A4, I, 575; also CAB 134/1557.
8. C.C. 52 (62) 1 August 1962. CAB 128/36/2.
9. C.C. 14 (64) 11 December 1964. CAB 128/39/1.
10. See *The Times*, especially leading article of 28 March 1958.
11. C.C. (62) 11. 6 February 1962. CAB 128/36/1.
12. *Keesing's Contemporary Archives* 1965–66, 21428.
13. C (53) 261. 30 September 1953. CAB 129/63.
14. C.C. 15 (62) 22 February 1962. CAB 128/36/1; see also C.M. 3 (63) 31 October 1963. CAB 128/38/1.
15. C.C. 44 (63) 4 July 1963. CAB 128/37.
16. C (53) 329. 21 November 1953. CAB 129/64.
17. C.M. 16 (56) 22 February 1956. CAB 128/30/1.
18. C.M. 25 (56) 27 March 1956. CAB 128/30/1.
19. C.C. 55 (61) 10 October 1961. CAB 128/35/2.
20. C.M. Turnbull, *A History of Singapore*, p. 278.
21. BDEE A4, I, v.57, 4–28.

11 Seeking a Role

1. At West Point Military Academy, 5 December 1962.
2. See John Darwin, *Britain and Decolonisation*, pp. 289–307; David McIntyre, *British Decolonization*, pp. 62–3.
3. Judith M. Brown and Wm. Roger Louis, in OHBE IV, p. 26.
4. C.M. 19 (55) 30 June 1955. CAB 128/29.
5. C.C. 41 (60) 13 July 1960. CAB 128/34.
6. C.C. 42 (61) 21 July 1961. CAB 128/35/2; and see C (61) 111, 21 July 1961. CAB 129/106.
7. C.C. 42 (61); also C (61) 104. 18 July 1961. CAB 129/106.
8. C.C. 42 (61); also C (61) 96. 1 July 1961. CAB 129/105.
9. C (61) 103. 18 July 1961. CAB 129/106.
10. C (61) 108. 19 July 1961. CAB 129/107.

11. C.C. 44 (61) 27 July 1961. CAB 128/35/2.
12. C. (62) 136. 27 August 1962. CAB 129/110.
13. C.C. 55 (62) 22 August 1962. CAB 128/36/2.
14. C.C. 56 (62) 13 September 1962. CAB 128/36/2.
15. C.C. 4 (63) 17 January 1963. CAB 128/37.
16. C.C. 10 (65) 18 February 1965. CAB 128/39/1.
17. C.C. 26, 27 (67) 30 April, 2 May 1967. CAB 128/42/2.
18. C. (67) 59. 24 April 1967. CAB 129/129/1.
19. C. (67) 63. 25 April 1967. CAB 129/129/1.
20. C.C. 56 (63) 23 September 1963. CAB 128/37.
21. C.C. 3 (63) 31 October 1963. CAB 128/38/1.
22. C.C. 3 (66) 25 January 1966. CAB 128/41/1.
23. C.C. 46 (66) 16 September 1966. CAB 128/41/2.
24. C.C. 66 (66) 13 December 1966. CAB 128/41/3.
25. C.C. 48 (66) 29 September 1966. CAB 128/41/3.
26. C.C. 64 (66) 6 December 1966. CAB 128/41/3.
27. C.C. 66 (66) 13 December 1966. CAB 128/41/3.
28. C.C. 50 (66) 13 October 1966. CAB 128/46.
29. Howard S. Levie, *The Status of Gibraltar*, pp. 30 *et seq.*
30. A good general account of the modern history of Gibraltar is given in D.S. Morris and R.H. Haigh, *Britain, Spain and Gibraltar 1945–90: The Eternal Triangle.*
31. C.C. 51 (66) 20 October 1966; C.C. 67 (66) 20 December 1966. CAB 128/41/3.
32. A summary of early events in the Falklands is given in G.D. Moir, *The History of the Falklands.*
33. C.C. 48 (66) 29 September 1966. CAB 128/41/3.
34. Nicholas J. White, *Decolonisation...*, p. 43.
35. C.C. 33 (67) 30 May 1967; C.C. 39 (67) 15 June 1967; C.C. 50 (67) 20 July 1967; C.C. 54 (67) 7 September 1967. CAB 128/42/2, 3.
36. John Darwin, *Britain and Decolonisation*, p. 310.

12 Reflections

1. W. David McIntyre, *British Decolonization...*, p. 22.
2. Rance to Listowel, 9 June 1947. Burma II, 574.
3. R.F. Holland, *European Decolonization...*, p. 27.
4. Holland, *op. cit.*, p. 5.
5. John Darwin, *Britain and Decolonisation*, p. 18.
6. See Nicholas J. White, *Decolonisation...*, passim.
7. Paul Johnson, *A History of the Modern World*, p. 539.
8. OHBE IV, p. 701.

Select Bibliography

Primary sources

British Documents on the End of Empire. HMSO.
Series A.
    Vol. 1:   Imperial Policy and Colonial Practice, 1925–1945.
    Parts I and II (1996).
    Vol. 2:   The Labour Government and the End of Empire, 1945–1951.
    Parts I, II, III and IV (1992).
    Vol. 3:   The Conservative Government and the End of Empire, 1951–1957.
    Parts I, II and III (1994).
    Vol. 4:   The Conservative Government and the End of Empire, 1957–1964.
    Parts I and II (2000).
Series B.
    Vol. 1:   Ghana.
    Parts I and II (1992).
    Vol. 2:   Sri Lanka.
    Parts I and II (1997).
    Vol. 3:   Malaya.
    Parts I and II (1995).
    Vol. 4:   Egypt and the defence of the Middle East.
    Parts I, II and III (1998).
    Vol. 5:   Sudan.
    Parts I and II (1998).
    Vol. 6:   West Indies.
    One part, 1999.
    Cited as BDEE A1, I, etc.
    Further volumes in preparation.
Cabinet Memoranda (1917–39) Public Record Office. CAB 24.
Cabinet Memoranda (1939–45) Public Record Office. CAB 66.
Cabinet Memoranda (1945–) Public Record Office. CAB 129.
Cabinet Minutes (1917–39) Public Record Office. CAB 23.
Cabinet Minutes (1939–45) Public Record Office. CAB 65.
Cabinet Minutes (1945–) Public Record Office. CAB 128.
Constitutional relations between Britain and Burma: Burma: the Struggle for Independence, 1944–1948. Editor Hugh Tinker. HMSO.
    Vol. I: 1.i.44–31.viii.46 (1983); Vol. II: 31.viii.46–4.i.48 (1984)
    Cited as Burma I, II.
Constitutional relations between Britain and India: The Transfer of Power 1942–47. Editor in chief Nicholas Mansergh. HMSO.

177

Vol. 1: i–iv 42 (1970); Vol. 2: 30.iv–21.ix.42 (1971); Vol. 3: 21.ix.42–12.vi.43 (1971); Vol. 4: 15.vi.43–31.viii.44 (1973); Vol. 5: 1.ix.44–28.vii.45 (1974); Vol. 6: 1.viii.45–22.iii.46; Vol. 7: 23.iii–29.vi.46 (1977); Vol. 8: 3.vii–1.xi.46 (1979); Vol. 9: 4.xi.46–22.iii.47 (1980); Vol. 10: 22.iii–30.v.47 (1981); Vol. 11: 31.v–7.vii.47 (1982); Vol. 12: 8.vii–15.viii.47 (1983)
Cited as *Transfer of Power* I, etc.
Premier papers, Public Record Office. PREM, various numbers.

Reference works

Commonwealth Year Book.
Dictionary of National Biography.
Encyclopedia Britannica.
Hansard (House of Commons and House of Lords).
Keesing's Contemporary Archives/Keesing's Record of World Events.
Mitchell, B.R., *International Historical Statistics: Africa, Asia, Oceania 1750–1993.* 3rd edn, Basingstoke: Macmillan – now Palgrave Macmillan, 1998.
Mitchell, B.R., *International Historical Statistics: The Americas 1750–1988.* 2nd edn, New York: Stockton Press, 1993.
Mitchell, B.R., *International Historical Statistics: Europe 1750–1993.* 4th edn, Basingstoke: Macmillan – now Palgrave Macmillan, 1998.
The Times.
United Nations Demographic Year Book.

Other sources

Adamson, David, *The Last Empire: Britain and the Commonwealth*, London: I.B. Tauris, 1989.
Alie, Joe A.D., *A New History of Sierra Leone*, New York: St. Martin's Press, 1990.
Annual Register.
Ashby, Sir Eric, *Universities: British, Indian, African: A Study in the Ecology of Higher Education*, London: Weidenfeld & Nicolson, 1966.
Blake, Robert, *A History of Rhodesia*, London: Eyre Methuen, 1977.
Boyce, D. George, *Decolonisation and the British Empire 1775–1997*, Basingstoke: Palgrave Macmillan 1999.
Brown, Judith M., *Modern India: The Origins of an Asian Democracy*, 2nd edn, Oxford: Oxford University Press, 1994.
Cain, P.J. and Hopkins, A.G., *British Imperialism: Crisis and Deconstruction 1914–1990*, London and New York: Longmans, 1993.
Churchill, Winston, *The Second World War*. Vol. 3: *The Grand Alliance*, London: Cassell, 1950.
Cohen, Michael J., *The Origins and Evolution of the British Empire, 1918–1968*, London: Hodder & Stoughton, 1968.
Cope, John, *South Africa*, London: Ernest Benn Ltd, 1965.

Cross, Colin, *The Fall of the Arab Zionist Conflict*, Berkeley: University. of California Press, 1987.

Darwin, John, *Britain and Decolonisation...*, Basingstoke: Macmillan – now Palgrave Macmillan, 1988.

Darwin, John, *The End of the British Empire*, Institute of Contemporary British History, Oxford: Blackwell, 1991.

Davies, Norman, *The Isles: A History*, Basingstoke: Macmillan – now Palgrave Macmillan, 1999.

Dawson, Robert MacGregor, *The Development of Dominion Status 1900–1936*, 2nd edn, London: Frank Cass, 1965.

Diamond, Larry, *Class, Ethnicity and Democracy in Nigeria*, London: Macmillan, 1968.

Donnison, F.S.V., *Burma*, London: Benn, 1970.

Draper, Alfred, *Amritsar: The Massacre that Ended the Raj*, London: Cassell, 1981.

Eden, Anthony (Earl of Avon), *The Eden Memoirs*. Vol. 3: *The Reckoning*, London: Cassell, 1965.

Edgerton, Robert B., *Mau Mau: An African crucible*, London: I.B. Tauris, 1990.

Edwardes, Michael, *The Last Days of British India*, London: Cassell, 1963.

Ezera, Kahi, *Constitutional Developments in Nigeria*, Cambridge: Cambridge University Press, 1964.

Fisher, Nigel, *Iain Macleod*, London: André Deutsch, 1973.

Gailey, Harry A., *A History of the Gambia*, London: Routledge & Kegan Paul, 1964.

Gilbert, Martin, *Winston S. Churchill* vol. 5 (1922–1939); vol. 6 (1939–41) London: Heinemann, 1976; 1983.

Goldblatt, I., *History of South-West Africa*, Cape Town, 1971.

Gullick, J.W., *Malaya*, 2nd edn, London: Macmillan, 1964.

Holland, R.F., *European Decolonization 1918–1981: An Introductory Survey*, Basingstoke: Macmillan, 1985.

Holt, P.W. and Daly, M.W., *A History of the Sudan from the Coming of Islam to the Present Day*, 4th edn, London and New York: Longman, 1988.

Htin Aung, Maung, *A History of Burma*, New York and London: Columbia University Press, 1967.

Johnson, Paul. *A History of the Modern World*. London: Weidenfeld and Nicolson.

Kennedy, J., *A History of Malaya*, 2nd edn, London: Macmillan, 1970.

Lapping, Brian, *End of Empire*, London: Granada Publishing, 1985.

Law, D.A., *Eclipse of Empire*, Cambridge: Cambridge University Press, 1993.

Levie, Howard S., *The Status of Gibraltar*, Boulder: Westview Press, 1982.

Lewis, I.M., *A Modern History of Somalia...*, 3rd edn, Boulder and London: Westview Press, 1988.

Lloyd, Selwyn, *Suez 1956: A Personal Account*, London: Jonathan Cape, 1978.

Lloyd, T.O., *The British Empire 1558–1995*, 2nd edn, Oxford: Oxford University Press, 1996.

McIntyre, W. David, *British Decolonization 1946–97*, Basingstoke: Macmillan – now Palgrave Macmillan, 1998.

Macmillan, Harold (Earl of Stockton), *Tides of Fortune 1945–1955*, London: Macmillan, 1969.

Macphee, A. Marshall, *Kenya*, London: Ernest Benn, 1968.

Mansfield, Peter, *The British in Egypt*, London: Weidenfeld & Nicolson, 1971.

Marquand, Leo, *The Peoples and Policies of South Africa*, 4th edn, Oxford: Oxford University Press, 1969.

Mitchell, B.R., *International Historical Statistics: Africa, Asia and Oceania, 1750–1993*, 3rd edn, Cambridge: Cambridge University Press, 1998.

Moir, G.D., *The History of the Falklands*, 2nd edn, Croydon, 1995.

Moon, P. (ed.): *Wavell: the Viceroy's Journal*, Oxford: Oxford University Press, 1973.

Morris, D.S. and Haigh, R.H., *Britain, Spain and Gibraltar 1945–90: The Eternal Triangle*, London and New York: Routledge, 1992.

Mutibwa, Phares, *Uganda since Independence...*, London: Hurst, 1992.

Nicolson, I.F., *The Administration of Nigeria 1900–1960...*, Oxford: Clarendon Press, 1969.

Nutting, Anthony, *No End of a Lesson: The Story of Suez*, London: Constable, 1967.

Oxford History of the British Empire, Vol. IV: The Twentieth Century, Judith M. Brown and Wm. Roger Louis, eds., Oxford: Oxford University Press, 1999. Cited as OHBE IV.

Palmer, Alan, *Dictionary of the British Empire and Commonwealth*, London: John Murray, 1996.

Petchenkine, Youry, *Ghana: In Search of Stability*, Westport, Conn. and London: Praeger, 1993.

Porter, A.N. and Stockwell, A.J., *British Imperial Policy and Decolonization 1938–64*, 2 vols., Basingstoke: Macmillan, 1987–88.

Rizvi, Gowhar, *Linlithgow and India: A Study of British Policy and the Political Impasse in India, 1936–43*, London: Royal Historical Society, 1978.

Royal Institute of International Affairs, *The British Empire: A Report on its Structure and Problems*, Oxford: Oxford University Press, 1939.

Royal Institute of International Affairs, *Great Britain and Palestine 1915–1945*, Westport, Conn.: Hyperion Press, 1976.

Ryan, N.J., *The Making of Modern Malaysia...*, Oxford: Oxford University Press, 1967.

Schlote, Werner, *British Overseas Trade from 1700 to the 1930s*, Oxford: Blackwell, 1952.

Schwarz, Walter, *Nigeria*, New York: Praeger, 1969.

Simon, Viscount, *Retrospect*, London: Hutchinson, 1952.

Toye, Hugh, *The Springing Tiger: A Study of a Revolutionary*, London: Cassell, 1955.

Tregonning, K.G., *A History of Modern Malaya*, London: Eastern University Press, 1962.

Turnbull, Constance Mary, *A History of Singapore*, Oxford: Oxford University Press, 1977.

Ward, W.E.F., *A History of Ghana*, 4th edn, London: George Allen & Unwin, 1967.

Welsh, Frank, *A History of Hong Kong*, London: Harper Collins, 1993.

White, Nicholas J., *Decolonisation: The British Experience since 1945*, London and New York: Longman, 1999.

Wood, J.R.T., *The Welensky Papers: A History of the Federation of Rhodesia and Nyasaland*, Durban: Graham, 1983.

Woodcock, George, *Who Killed the British Empire?*, London: Jonathan Cape, 1974.

Yeager, Rodger, *Tanzania: An African Experiment*, Boulder: Westview Press, 1982.

Ziegler, Philip, *Mountbatten: The Official Biography*, London: Collins, 1985.

Index